A Retreat With Anthony of Padua

Other titles in the A Retreat With... Series:

A RETREAT WITH
ANTHONY OF PADUA

Finding Our Way

Carol Ann Morrow

ST. ANTHONY MESSENGER PRESS

Cincinnati, Ohio

The excerpt from *The Stone Diaries*, by Carol Shields, copyright ©1993 by Carol Shields, is used by permission of Viking Penguin, a division of Penguin Putnam Inc.

The excerpt from *Angela's Ashes*, by Frank McCourt, copyright ©1996, is reprinted by permission of HarperCollins Publishers Ltd.

Scripture citations are taken from the *New Revised Standard Version Bible*, copyright ©1989 by the Division of Christian Education of the National Council of Churches of Christ in the U.S.A. and used by permission.

Cover illustration by Steve Erspamer, S.M.
Cover and book design by Mary Alfieri
Electronic format and pagination by Sandy L. Digman

ISBN 0-86716-310-0

Published by St. Anthony Messenger Press
Printed in the U.S.A.

TO FATHER NORMAN PERRY, O.F.M.
who enkindled my affection
for Anthony
and supported
and shared
my quest to know more of him.
Father Norman mirrors Anthony to me
in his own Franciscan life,
in his love of the written word
and in his breadth of knowledge
balanced with compassion.

Contents

Introducing A Retreat With...

Twenty years ago I made a weekend retreat at a Franciscan house on the coast of New Hampshire. The retreat director's opening talk was as lively as a long-range weather forecast. He told us how completely God loves each one of us—without benefit of lively anecdotes or fresh insights.

As the friar rambled on, my inner critic kept up a *sotto voce* commentary: "I've heard all this before." "Wish he'd say something new that I could chew on." "That poor man really doesn't have much to say." Ever hungry for manna yet untasted, I devalued any experience of hearing the same old thing.

After a good night's sleep, I awoke feeling as peaceful as a traveler who has at last arrived safely home. I walked across the room toward the closet. On the way I passed the sink with its small framed mirror on the wall above. Something caught my eye like an unexpected presence. I turned, saw the reflection in the mirror and said aloud, "No wonder he loves me!"

This involuntary affirmation stunned me. What or whom had I seen in the mirror? When I looked again, it was "just me," an ordinary person with a lower-than-average reservoir of self-esteem. But I knew that in the initial vision I had seen God-in-me breaking through like a sudden sunrise.

At that moment I knew what it meant to be made in the divine image. I understood right down to my size eleven feet what it meant to be loved exactly as I was.

Only later did I connect this revelation with one granted to the Trappist monk-writer Thomas Merton. As he reports in *Conjectures of a Guilty Bystander*, while standing all unsuspecting on a street corner one day, he was overwhelmed by the "joy of being...a member of a race in which God Himself became incarnate.... There is no way of telling people that they are all walking around shining like the sun."

As an absentminded homemaker may leave a wedding ring on the kitchen windowsill, so I have often mislaid this precious conviction. But I have never forgotten that particular retreat. It persuaded me that the Spirit rushes in where it will. Not even a boring director or a judgmental retreatant can withstand the "violent wind" that "fills the entire house" where we dwell in expectation (see Acts 2:2).

So why deny ourselves any opportunity to come aside awhile and rest on holy ground? Why not withdraw from the daily web that keeps us muddled and wound? Wordsworth's complaint is ours as well: "The world is too much with us." There is no flu shot to protect us from infection by the skepticism of the media, the greed of commerce, the alienating influence of technology. We need retreats as the deer needs the running stream.

An Invitation

This book and its companions in the *A Retreat With...* series from St. Anthony Messenger Press are designed to meet that need. They are an invitation to choose as director some of the most powerful, appealing and wise mentors our faith tradition has to offer.

Our directors come from many countries, historical eras and schools of spirituality. At times they are teamed to sing in close harmony (for example, Francis de Sales, Jane de Chantal and Aelred of Rievaulx on spiritual friendship). Others are paired to kindle an illuminating fire from the friction of their differing views (such as Augustine of Hippo and Mary Magdalene on human sexuality). All have been chosen because, in their humanness and their holiness, they can help us grow in self-knowledge, discernment of God's will and maturity in the Spirit.

Inviting us into relationship with these saints and holy ones are inspired authors from today's world, women and men whose creative gifts open our windows to the Spirit's flow. As a motto for the authors of our series, we have borrowed the advice of Dom Frederick Dunne to the young Thomas Merton. Upon joining the Trappist monks, Merton wanted to sacrifice his writing activities lest they interfere with his contemplative vocation. Dom Frederick wisely advised, "Keep on writing books that make people love the spiritual life."

That is our motto. Our purpose is to foster (or strengthen) friendships between readers and retreat directors—friendships that feed the soul with wisdom, past and present. Like the scribe "trained for the kingdom of heaven," each author brings forth from his or her storeroom "what is new and what is old" (Matthew 13:52).

The Format

The pattern for each *A Retreat With...* remains the same; readers of one will be in familiar territory when they move on to the next. Each book is organized as a seven-session retreat that readers may adapt to their own schedules or to the needs of a group.

Day One begins with an anecdotal introduction called "Getting to Know Our Directors." Readers are given a telling glimpse of the guides with whom they will be sharing the retreat experience. A second section, "Placing Our Directors in Context," will enable retreatants to see the guides in their own historical, geographical, cultural and spiritual settings.

Having made the human link between seeker and guide, the authors go on to "Introducing Our Retreat Theme." This section clarifies how the guide(s) are especially suited to explore the theme and how the retreatant's spirituality can be nourished by it.

After an original "Opening Prayer" to breathe life into the day's reflection, the author, speaking with and through the mentor(s), will begin to spin out the theme. While focusing on the guide(s)' own words and experience, the author may also draw on Scripture, tradition, literature, art, music, psychology or contemporary events to illuminate the path.

Each day's session is followed by reflection questions designed to challenge, affirm and guide the reader in integrating the theme into daily life. A "Closing Prayer" brings the session full circle and provides a spark of inspiration for the reader to harbor until the next session.

Days Two through Six begin with "Coming Together in the Spirit" and follow a format similar to Day One. Day Seven weaves the entire retreat together, encourages a continuation of the mentoring relationship and concludes with "Deepening Your Acquaintance," an envoi to live the theme by God's grace, the director(s)' guidance and the retreatant's discernment. A closing section of Resources serves as a larder from which readers may draw enriching books, videos, cassettes and films.

We hope readers will experience at least one of those memorable "No wonder God loves me!" moments. And we hope that they will have "talked back" to the mentors, as good friends are wont to do.

A case in point: There was once a famous preacher who always drew a capacity crowd to the cathedral. Whenever he spoke, an eccentric old woman sat in the front pew directly beneath the pulpit. She took every opportunity to mumble complaints and contradictions— just loud enough for the preacher to catch the drift that he was not as wonderful as he was reputed to be. Others seated down front glowered at the woman and tried to shush her. But she went right on needling the preacher to her heart's content.

When the old woman died, the congregation was astounded at the depth and sincerity of the preacher's grief. Asked why he was so bereft, he responded, "Now who will help me to grow?"

All of our mentors in *A Retreat With...* are worthy guides. Yet none would seek retreatants who simply said, "Where you lead, I will follow. You're the expert." In truth, our directors provide only half the retreat's content. Readers themselves will generate the other half.

As general editor for the retreat series, I pray that readers will, by their questions, comments, doubts and decision-making, fertilize the seeds our mentors have planted.

And may the Spirit of God rush in to give the growth.

Gloria Hutchinson
Series Editor
Conversion of Saint Paul, 1995

Getting to Know Our Director

You want to know who I am? It is the work of a lifetime. I believe the way of holiness is to learn one's path and follow it—over land and sea if necessary. And I have been so very lost! I have been lost at sea, I have been lost on solid ground.

But now I am here and I am willing to share my losses and my discoveries with you. I am Friar Anthony. I follow the way of Brother Francis of Assisi. They call him the Little Poor Man. Perhaps some call me the Big Poor Man. I am larger by far than my spiritual father but I, too, want to be a simple, traveling preacher. And that is why you've come, isn't it, to hear me preach from my heart what Francis has taught me of the gospel.

I want to know you as well. I want to be at home with you, to discover what moves you, touches you, what brings you here. But first you want to know who it is who is searching for answers with you during this retreat. So I'll tell you a little of my story.

I was not always called Anthony. I was born Fernando Bulhom in Lisbon, Portugal, in 1195 or perhaps a little earlier—it matters little. Our family home was very near to the cathedral church, which did matter. My parents were fairly well-off. When I was about fifteen, I already knew I wanted to live where the Gospels were honored and I became an Augustinian at St. Vincent's Outside the Walls. Being outside the walls didn't isolate St. Vincent's from the capital city's bustle, though, so I later asked to be transferred to Santa Cruz in Coimbra.

I thought Coimbra might be more tranquil, but when I arrived I still felt like I was outside—separated from something essential to my soul's journey. Coimbra was the intellectual center of Portugal, though, and I feasted on the volumes in the monastery library, learning much.

Then our monastery was given the honor to house the remains of the first Franciscan martyrs. It was a political decision to give Santa Cruz these precious relics, but it had spiritual repercussions for me. Perhaps some of you have visited the twentieth-century gravesite of Martin Luther King, Jr., in Atlanta, the Vietnam War Memorial in Washington, D.C., or another place made holy by the presence of someone you love. Do you remember the vitality of your spiritual connection to those people, those events? That is how I felt when I saw those martyrs' bones. That is what I wanted: I wanted to risk everything to speak the words of Jesus.

But Santa Cruz Monastery was home to men who had grown comfortable, even careless with the gospel. The bones of the first five Franciscan martyrs would dry and crumble there, and be gathered into little reliquaries. I wanted to live in Ezekiel's valley where the bones of the martyrs could rise up and prophesy anew. When the Franciscans, new to Portugal in 1220, came to our door begging, I begged for the privilege of joining them. I wanted to take my own young bones as soon as possible to preach to the Saracens.

How could the Moroccan people who had so influenced my homeland, who knew so much of beauty and adventure, how could they not know Jesus as I did? My own risk seemed so small to buy so great a treasure for a whole people.

I may seem impetuous to you. Sometimes I seem so to myself. But, once again, I left a safe place for the open road, to find my way. The friars were new to Portugal, new to the Church, new to me. But the gospel was their compass and I knew they would lead me in a direction good for my soul.

In Morocco, I preached not a single word, humbled by a body martyred only by illness, not by scimitars. When I felt well enough to sail back to Portugal, storms blew our ship all the way to Sicily instead—far, far from my homeland but near to the home of my spiritual father. All of us Franciscans were itinerants of a sort, so I've been on the road ever since.

My work was to help ordinary people puzzled by preachers who had either chosen or stumbled into heresies. I was to reason with, inspire, bless and lead them. Today I might be compared to a politician on the campaign trail—only my campaign was simply to use my knowledge of many things to help people make spiritual connections.

I lived in Europe's Middle Ages, when the style of preaching and teaching, the worldview and the social climate were very different from what you've experienced. You may find that my words—as written— seem florid and heavy. But when I spoke, I lit a fire in people's hearts. How else could I have gathered audiences so large that they couldn't fit in the largest church but had to sit in fields and meadows?

So I've told you the circuitous path I took from Lisbon, Portugal, to Padua, Italy, by way of Morocco and Sicily. Now I'd like you to know what that world was like.

Placing Our Director in Context

I lived in what is now called the High Middle Ages— a time of social and religious upheaval, chaos and new beginnings.

My native country is Portugal, recognized as an independent nation by the pope in 1179. I was born in Lisbon during the reign of Sancho I, Portugal's second king. Legend says that Lisbon was founded by the Greek hero Odysseus. Sometimes I feel that I followed his star of travel and adventure in my own life. Before my time, my homeland had often been under the control of the African Moors. King Sancho extended Portugal's borders with the help of the Knights Templar and other crusaders. The king encouraged religious life, founding monasteries such as the one in which I came to live.

The Canons Regular of St. Augustine differed from monks in that we worked as pastors, connecting to the world outside our monastery through preaching and works of charity.

While I was at Santa Cruz Monastery in Coimbra, the people of Castile (now part of Spain) definitively ended the power of the Almohads (a Muslim power). Coimbra was then the nation's capital and our Portuguese queen consort, sister of the victorious Castilian leader, came to Santa Cruz to express her thanks in public prayer.

Although our Holy Father Francis of Assisi is, I am sure, better known to most people now, Emperor Frederick II and Pope Innocent III were the more powerful in my lifetime. It was Innocent who approved Francis' way of life. He believed in his authority over political rulers and exercised it with some success. Within the Church, he called the Fourth Lateran Council, which struggled with heresy and legislated the reception of the sacraments, two areas which later touched my life and mission.

Innocent also called for a crusade against the Albigensian heresy and the Fourth Crusade to the Holy Land. The Crusaders recaptured Jerusalem in 1229, though it was lost again some years after my death.

Italy, with which I am most often identified, was my
home only for little over a decade. At the time I lived
there, Rome was the capital of the Papal States and what
you now call Italy was linked mostly by geography.
Venice, so near my Padua, was the link between Europe
and the Orient and the launching point for many
crusaders.

Italy held many walled and fortified cities, little
princes and small tyrants. Padua is said to be the oldest
city in the country. Its university is the country's oldest.
Universities were new in my lifetime, not only in Portugal
and Italy, but in all the known world.

You should also know that the times in which I lived
saw a transition from an agrarian, barter economy to a
merchant, cash economy. This movement to the city with
its trades, crafts and guilds was not a smooth one. The
numbers of the poor increased drastically. Many people
had never owned land. Those who did sometimes had to
sell it for cash. When they were out of cash, they had to
borrow. If crops were bad or they became ill, the interest
mounted, and they lost any hope of regaining their
foothold. They became permanently poor, many of them
living on the edge of forests, foraging, begging, eking out
a precarious existence.

Religion was the warp and woof weaving the days
and nights of medieval life together and influencing the
life of the nation. Religion was the first and most public
motive of the Crusades, although I wouldn't have you
think they were only about faith. This was the world in
which Francis of Assisi founded the Order of Friars Minor
and, later, the Poor Clares and the lay Third Order, whose
members were not to fight in these many skirmishes
between cities. This was the world into which I came,
more educated than the man I elected to follow, more
cosmopolitan, one might say, but just as eager to bring

Jesus to those who had yet to know of him.

This is the world in which I spent just thirty-six years—not so short a life by the standards of the time. It is the setting in which I found all that I wish to share with you now.

Day One
Finding the Way

Introducing Our Retreat Theme

I have a reputation among you, one beyond even my understanding, though I am called Doctor of the Church. I am petitioned and praised as the finder of what is lost. I am not sure that I deserve your kind esteem for helping people to find their keys, their rings, their many valuables, but this need has drawn many to seek me out.

My talent, if I dare claim it, does have its roots in an actual event. When I was traveling in France during the years 1224-1227, I spent time in Montpellier with my brother novices. Books were scarce and certainly too valuable for us poor friars to own. Since I walked from place to place, I would have been quite weighed down by even a few manuscripts! Still, I did carry with me a text of the Psalms and in its margins I had written notes which helped me to point out parallels with other Scripture passages.

"One night, a newly received novice decided to leave and took with him the manuscript."[1] I prayed that this young man might have a change of heart and indeed, he stopped at the bridge over the River Herault and turned back. He not only returned the text with my notes, but he also found new heart for following the Franciscan way.

I invite you to come on a treasure hunt with me these

seven days. I want you to experience my "gift" for
finding what is lost. I want you to experience your own
lostness as well as recall your losses large and small in the
world of possessing and being possessed. And I want you
to know the joy of being found.

You have this expression in your life and times, "I
need to find myself." Yet, just like my retreatants in 1231,
you have tried to find yourself by acquisitions, by
"making your mark," by making an impression. Of all the
things I am petitioned to find, I want most for you to find
yourself—in God.

Opening Prayer

Jesus, who came to seek the lost,
give me the willingness
to be found
by you.

I am scattered about,
playing hide and seek with grace.

Pieces of my self
lie here and there,
in this room and that,
in the past and over the horizon,
above and below,
within and without.

Gather me together
as a mother hen
gathers her chicks.
I want to be under your wing,
where your heartbeat
and mine can sound as one.

I trust you to lead me
with gentleness
to my heart's core.

Retreat Session One
Search and You Will Find

I know you wish to learn from me, from my words,
from my life. So I must warn you immediately: At times, I
am myself unable to sift out my own thoughts and
inspirations from the words of Scripture. Rumor has it
that I know the Bible by heart[2] and that, were the Bible to
be lost, you could piece it together from my sermons. To
that, I can only say that it would surely be a shorter book,
to judge from the thickness of my own work!

Yet the Word of God has indeed shaped my own
words and settled so deeply in my heart that, when I
speak, I also hear the prophets, the psalmist, the
evangelists as well as Peter, Paul and James in the words
of my mouth. I fear that you may be so familiar with
these words that you may allow your eyes to glimpse
them and glide over them without tasting their
sweetness, without hearing their daily challenge.

What can I say to you? I see myself like the faithful
Ruth in the fields, gleaning behind the harvesters,
gathering every grain and using it to feed my spiritual
hunger—and that of you, my family.[3] Please take and eat.

When I look back at the activity of God in my life, the
Bible gives me words to describe it. This same Word of
God holds your story as well. I want to trace the
movement of the Spirit in the searches of my early life
simply to illustrate how you can also find your life

documented and illuminated in this Holy Book.

'Search, and you will find'

I did not have to seek far to find my first spiritual
home with the Augustinians at Sao Vicente de Fora.
Though it was outside the city walls, it was quite near my
parents' home in the port city of Lisbon. People will tell
you I was quite young but let me assure you that I was
already on a quest.

And you can tell me, I'm sure, of the ideals of your
own youth—how you played games in which you were
the priest, the teacher, the parent, the leader. I wanted to
find the answers, know the purpose of creation,
understand life's meaning. Sao Vicente had an excellent
library. I read much and I was taught by well-educated
monks, one of whom was also a great orator.

Yet something I felt in my heart to be central to
monastic life was missing—silence. Two years were
enough to know: I requested a transfer to Santa Cruz
Monastery in Coimbra, to the north and further inland. I
studied nine years at Santa Cruz. Like Saint Augustine,
whose works the Augustinians revered and studied, my
heart was restless. My teachers were intelligent and well-
educated, but they were not holy.

Dared I change once again? In the Gospel of Matthew,
Chapter Seven challenged me. I am not to judge. I read,
"First take the log out of your own eye."[4] I was not sure I
could keep my vision clear at Santa Cruz. I was young.
But I asked, I sought, I knocked[5] and—just as promised—
my heavenly Father gave good things to me, Anthony, the
seeker.

The first Franciscans to visit our monastery were
dead ones: the martyrs, whose bones were brought as
valuable relics to Santa Cruz. That was my introduction

to the Little Poor Men, followers of Francis of Assisi, and new to our fledgling nation. My vision was finding me, it seemed. Who has knocked at the door of your heart? What words of Scripture come to rest in you when you are still?

'What do I still lack?'

I was the young man Matthew describes in Chapter 19 of his Gospel. I kept asking, "What good deed must I do...?"[6] and "What do I still lack?"[7] I knew the answer he had been given. But what did I have to sell? What could I give away?

I had already given everything—except what I was learning at Santa Cruz: the Holy Bible, first of all, but also Augustine, Bede, Aristotle, Jerome, Cicero, Gregory, Pliny, Isidore and Bernard of Clairvaux. I studied natural history, etymology, anatomy and theology. I heard "Go, sell your possessions...then come, follow me"[8] and I leaped at the answer to my questions. Perhaps it was that day I was convinced that what I possessed was a gift for unfolding the Scriptures to anyone who would listen. I gained the courage to request transfer to the itinerant, unlettered Franciscans.

I have found that the words of the Gospel are not so much a spice as a leaven. They work inside a person until they effect a change. They ask a question that pushes and probes and pokes. What has the Gospel asked of you? What have you answered?

'You brought up my life from the pit'

I thought that I could give my treasures of knowledge and faith away in Morocco, where those brave, foolish, first Franciscan martyrs had died. I traveled there but arrived so ill that I couldn't even get up out of bed to "announce the word of God," as Francis our founder told us to do. I was so sick that I scarcely knew that an entire season passed. I who read the Scriptures now read the book of those days with sorrow. Obviously, I was not meant to stay in Morocco. It was time to return to Portugal, to the little St. Anthony Friary, named for Anthony of Egypt, after whom I had taken my new name.

But my puny plan was not to be. Our ship was tossed about and unable to regain the Straits of Gibraltar. The Mediterranean spit us out like seaweed at the Straits of Messina instead, on the island of Sicily. Like Jonah, I prayed: "I called to the LORD out of my distress,/ and he answered me; / out of the belly of Sheol I cried / and you heard my voice. /...you brought up my life from the pit, O LORD, my God."[9]

Italy was home to my spiritual father Francis. And my Franciscan brothers were gathering in the valley of Umbria, far north of Sicily, to pray and talk about the future—my future as well. I felt ill, but the magnetism of Francis drew me on that long journey, more than halfway up the length of a land where an unfamiliar people spoke an unfamiliar language. Like Jonah, I held a message for the people. Unlike Jonah, I loved this land and these people. Perhaps I had finally found my place.

Have you ever been dumped, spit out, in a place—geographical or spiritual—you had not chosen? Are you in such a place today? What is the gift of this place for you? Know that you were not, are not, there by accident.

'I am gentle and humble of heart'

Not by accident did I have the grace of becoming a hermit. I joined the community of Franciscans at Montepaolo, near Forli, roughly midway between Assisi and Padua. It was midway in my life as well. Such a blessing was mine: to celebrate the Lord's Supper with the friars and live according to the guidance Francis himself had set out for hermitages. My first biographer is right to tell you: "He neither mentioned his studies nor boasted of the churchly ministry he had exercised; instead, out of love for Christ, hiding all his knowledge and intelligence, he declared that he wished to know, thirst for, and embrace only Christ...."[10]

It may not seem humble to cite a text about myself, but the friar who wrote this short life caught my motive, which is what I wish to share with you. Whatever I had studied, whatever I knew, was nothing. Like Paul writes in his letter to the Philippians, I wanted "to know Christ and the power of his resurrection and the sharing of his sufferings by becoming like him in his death."[11]

It did not seem to me that education and learning had brought this spiritual knowledge to the monks of Lisbon and Coimbra. The Franciscan friars, though uneducated, knew Christ. What a gift to discover that my past and my present were of a piece, that all my life was, and would continue to be, divinely led.

I went with my brothers to nearby Forli to celebrate ordinations and, there, I was asked to speak. (I must tell you that they had asked everyone else first and were truly desperate. Sometimes my brothers did not plan these festive occasions very well!)

I agreed with reluctance and my words, inspired by the Spirit, were so well received that the friar in charge of our province immediately assigned me the role of public preacher. I had treasured my hermit's life, seeing it as the way to be "gentle and humble of heart."[12] Now I saw that the yoke Jesus describes in the eleventh chapter of Matthew was the same as that which he took up at nearly the same age as me: a preaching ministry to the common people. What could I say but yes?

Are there Scripture passages that make you uncomfortable? Do you wish that some lines had not been written? Are you willing to spend some time with those passages, praying to know their meaning for you? I warn you: They may cause you to make a turn in the road! This I know!

Humility is one quality you will need to know your direction in life. Once I preached on Genesis 28:12, which describes Jacob's dream at Bethel, a dream in which he received direction. I wrote, "The ladder in Jacob's dream has two sidepieces and six rungs on which one can climb to the top. This ladder symbolizes Jesus Christ. The two sidepieces are his two natures: divine and human. The six rungs are Christ's six virtues: humility, poverty, wisdom, mercy, patience and obedience.... Behold the ladder stands ready even today. Why do you hesitate to climb it?"[13]

Hesitate no longer! Your path is present to you when you look with eyes of faith.

For Reflection

You are blessed to have your own copy of the Bible. The people with whom I spent my years in Italy and France depended on me to proclaim the word which they needed for direction and guidance. I invite you to seek out your own word today.

- **A Favorite Word:** *When you are at rest and seek a word from the Bible, what passage comes to you without even opening the book? The story of the young man pushes and probes and pokes me. It is a question that Pope John Paul II also finds challenging and a text on which he likes to preach.[14] Look for questions in the four Gospels. What does the gospel ask of you today? What will you answer?*

- **A Descriptive Word:** *What is a chapter or verse that describes your life at this time? Or, do you need—as I did—more than one to name different life passages you have experienced?*

- **A Difficult Word:** *Choose a Scripture passage or a part of the life of Christ that makes you uncomfortable. Read the passage with new willingness to accept its message for you.*

- **A Necessary Word:** *Climb Jacob's ladder to find a quality the Spirit can nurture in you during this retreat. To me, the six rungs of the ladder are humility, poverty, wisdom, mercy, patience and obedience. In Genesis 28, the ladder is actually a stairway, however, and its steps are not numbered. I have told you what the scene inspires in me. What does it inspire in you? What are the steps you must take to direct your life toward what is good, what is holy?*

Closing Prayer

We beseech you, Lord Jesus,
that in the seven brief days of this life
you help us to conceive the spirit of salvation
and bring to birth through a sorrowful heart
an heir to eternal life.
May we merit to drink from the river of living water
and rejoice together with you in heavenly Jerusalem.
Grant us this, you, who are blessed, glorious,
    laudable, lovable, sweet, and immortal through all
    centuries. And let every creature shout: Amen.
Alleluia.

—*Prayer of Saint Anthony*[15]

Notes

[1] Sophronius Clasen, O.F.M., trans. Ignatius Brady, O.F.M., *St. Anthony, Doctor of the Church* (Chicago: Franciscan Herald Press, 1973), p. 36.

[2] Rev. Louis Rohr, O.F.M., S.T.L., *The Use of Sacred Scripture in the Sermons of St. Anthony of Padua* (Washington, D.C.: The Catholic University of America Press, 1948), p. 24.

[3] See George Marcil, O.F.M., ed. and trans., *Anthony of Padua: Sermones for the Easter Cycle* (St. Bonaventure, N.Y.: The Franciscan Institute, 1994), p. 64.

[4] Matthew 7:5.

[5] Matthew 7:7.

[6] Matthew 19:16.

[7] Matthew 19:20.

[8] Matthew 19:21.

[9] Jonah 2:3,7.

[10] Bernard Przewozny, O.F.M. Conv. trans., *Life of St. Anthony: Assidua or Vita Prima* (Padua, Italy: Edizioni Messaggero, 1984), p. 9.

[11] Philippians 3:10.

[12] Matthew 11:29.

[13] Claude M. Jarmak, O.F.M. Conv., trans. in collaboration with Thomas E. Hunt, *Saint Anthony, Herald of the Good News: Excerpts from the Sermones of Saint Anthony* (Ellicott City, Md.: Conventual Franciscan Friars, 1995), p. 174.

[14] See Catholic News Service, ed., *John Paul II Speaks to Youth at World Youth Day* (Washington, D.C.: Catholic News Service, 1993).

[15] Marcil, p. 147.

DAY TWO

Finding Holy Ground

Coming Together in the Spirit

I will arise and go now, and go to Innisfree,
And a small cabin build there,
  of clay and wattles made:
Nine bean-rows will I have there,
  a hive for the honey-bee,
And live alone in the bee-loud glade.
And I shall have some peace there, for peace comes
  dropping slow....

—W.B. Yeats[1]

Knowing the direction we must go is but the first stage of
the spiritual search. As a poet closer to your time, William
Butler Yeats, says, "I will arise and go now." But Yeats
does not travel forever. He finds a place that speaks to his
heart and he settles in, confident that peace will be
"dropping from the veils of the morning to where the
cricket sings."[2]

Defining Our Thematic Context

My experience is like that of the much-later Yeats. I
traveled long, I traveled hard. I felt sea terrors and land
loneliness. But I was blessed to discover more than one

place that spoke to "the deep heart's core," as Yeats described his isle. You, too, need such a place, your own Bethlehem where you can be born and reborn, cradled and lullabied. I want to help you find that heart's home.

During my short life, I found two such places: an early cabin or cell (of which I spoke when we last met), and a later refuge outside Padua. Stretched between those two peaceful places my quest for holy ground found me often on the road. Perhaps you, too, are often on the road, looking behind for the cave you have left. You may be thinking that peace is where you have been in the long-ago distance, not where you are.

Francis of Assisi said that we carry our cloister with us. He, too, had his cave and his special retreats, but he and my spiritual brothers taught me to build not so much spiritual castles in the air but rather to erect spiritual shelters, oases by the roadside. Let me help you to locate or perhaps to prepare a blueprint—for the shelter you require.

Opening Prayer

I will arise and go now
to a place you have prepared.
I will arise with confidence
that I know the way
though your leading is revealed
just one step at a time.

You had no place
to lay your head
yet every place is yours,
marked by your miracles,
touched by your hand,
shaped by your love.

I will lay my head in your lap
and learn your leading.
I shall have much peace there
for peace comes dropping slow.

I will remain still
in this familiar place
and I will know it
for the first time.

Your welcome encompasses me,
Lord my God.
I know my place
and it is here
with you.

Retreat Session Two
In Your Deep Heart's Core

When I pray over and preach the Resurrection of
Jesus, which I love to do, I like to remember all the times
and places where the risen Lord appeared to those who
loved him. I count ten appearances[3] and none of them are
to strangers. Jesus appeared where he felt welcome.

You need to make such a welcome place also. You
could stumble upon it and claim it. You may design and
build it. You might visit such a place and, ever after, be
able to go there in your imagination. All these are
possible and desirable. When you find this place, you will
be like Isaac, to whom God said, "...settle in the land that
I shall show you. Reside in this land...and I will be with
you and will bless you."[4]

Pay Attention

My earliest biographer tells the story of my first claim to holy ground: "While Anthony was staying in that hermitage, a certain friar built himself a cell in a grotto [cave] which was suitable for prayer and where he could dedicate himself more freely to God. When [Anthony] saw it one day and realized how appropriate it was for growth in devotion, he went to entreat the friar and humbly asked him to cede to him the use of that cell. At last, when he obtained the place of peace, the servant of God, after fulfilling the morning community prayers, would daily retire to the cell, taking with himself some bread and a small container of water. In this way, he spent the day alone, forcing the body to serve the spirit...."[5] This happened in 1221 in Montepaolo, northwest of Firenze (Florence).

I cite this tale of how I was a spiritual squatter to show you the grace of a good example. I saw the good accomplished in my brother friar and longed to gain that good for myself. I paid attention. The cost of attention is high but so are the dividends.

Look around you to see what benefits the spiritual growth of your friends. Where do they go? What choices do they make? Where do they worship? Who counsels them?

Now look within. Where have you felt God's presence most deeply? Is it a place you can visit often? Is there "a place of peace" in your own home? Might you claim a quiet corner as your "cell"? What assists you in the movement toward peace? Are you more ready to enter a place others have already acknowledged as holy or would you like to create a new "chapel" or cell that you will consecrate as your own?

I took nourishment with me. What nourishes you?

The Scriptures? The fragrance of a candle or incense? An image that speaks of the divine? A prayer rug or pillow? The strains of music or the sounds of nature?

It is not my way to collect too many accessories for the prayer of a simple person. Nonetheless, I know that I lived in times where most people were poor and illiterate. You come with more resources as well as more potential distractions. Finding your holy ground requires you to sort out which is which.

In my Easter sermon, I note that Mary Magdalene was the first to see the risen Lord. "The grace of the Lord manifests itself first to a repentant soul."[6] Mary was at the tomb "early on the first day of the week, while it was still dark."[7] She knew where she needed to be to experience the presence of God. Where is that for you?

Stake a Claim

I "obtained the place of peace" by asking. I was blessed that my brother appreciated and acknowledged my hunger for this holy place. It is not enough to *know* what your holy place might include or where it might be located. You need to *express* in words or action your spiritual claim on the territory.

The second appearance of Jesus is to the women returning from the tomb. They had put themselves in the right place to see the risen Lord. The angels invited them: "Come and see the place where he lay."[8] To them, Jesus says, "Do not be afraid!"[9] You need to sit, kneel or prostrate yourself in the place you have claimed as holy and watch. The one who appeared to the women— faithful persons much like you—says to you as well, "I know that you are looking"[10] and "you will see him."[11]

Annie Dillard, a writer of your own times, knows much about finding holy ground. In *Pilgrim at Tinker*

Creek, she writes, "Experiencing the present purely is being emptied and hollow; you catch grace as a man fills his cup under a waterfall."[12] She is describing both my cave and your space and she knows that your cupped spirit, your posture of willingness, is crucial. You must not only know the location of your holy place, but you must also be there—emptied and hollow.

Keep Frequent Vigil

Three of the ten appearances of Jesus after the Resurrection were in the room made holy by Jesus bowing to wash the feet of his chosen family, his sharing of Passover with them and his final extended message of love. "For the Lord appears to those who recline in the upper room of their minds, that is, to those who withdraw from the rush of secular affairs."[13]

In Acts 1:4, during one of those visits, Jesus "told them not to leave Jerusalem: 'Wait, rather, for the fulfillment of my Father's promise.'" It is this constancy, this faithful showing up that blessed and strengthened me so much. I wish to encourage it in you. You must not only show up but you must also recline. "Must" is not a rule, but rather a truth of the soul. It is a part of what hallows the ground, this dedication to being present.

And, if you are present, the Presence will come. Annie Dillard calls it "stalking." She spends nearly an hour watching a muskrat and writes, "I never knew I was there either. For that forty minutes last night I was as purely sensitive and mute as a photographic plate."[14]

In my day, we had no such miracle as photographic plates, but we had much for which we waited. We lived by the seasons in ways you may not be able to imagine. We longed for the harvest. We longed for the rain—and for its end. We knew waiting but still needed the patience that makes it bearable.

The waiting requires our patience and learning patience requires that we wait. It is the spinning of a holy circle with you and God together at the center; it is the creation of an upper room.

You cannot postpone this waiting until you have nothing else to do. You must visit your holy space, you must ground yourself so that all your other actions emerge from your "deep heart's core." If you are grounded in the holy, then the Father's promise can come to fullness in you and be expressed by you wherever you are.

Sometimes people think that it was easy for the saints to be as photographic plates, sensitive and mute. Let me remind you of my wrenching moves from one religious order to another, from one country to another, from one way of life to another, in search of the ground where I could know the holy. I would not wish such struggles for you, but I suspect that you will know them nonetheless.

Appreciate your cell of silence and go there when it is easy, so that its magnetic field will still draw you when the days are difficult. You can fill it as a spiritual reservoir so that you can draw from its fullness when you are dry.

How can you be faithful to the vigil? Put it first in your day. Then it cannot be crowded out by the day's demands. This was my practice. I know that some of you do not greet the morning with joy. Find your own morning then. It will most often be at a transition time in your day: the move from home to work, the move from morning to afternoon, afternoon to evening, evening to rest.

Respect the rhythms of your body and your life. "Withdrawing" is the movement I encourage in you, the cessation of rushing, the claiming of your ground. I will have more to say of this on other days, since space and time are related dimensions of our lives.

Carry Your House in Your Heart

When I was an Augustinian, I was "attached" to a certain house. This was characteristic of the Rule, but perhaps you have experienced something similar in your own life. If you have followed my earlier advice, you may have even begun to attach yourself to a place. You have noticed the characteristics of such places for others, you have staked a claim and you grounded yourself in your space, retiring there on a regular basis.

Now I am going to tell you to take it all, to roll up your blueprint, pack up your spiritual tent and head for the road! Yes, groundedness in a place is a good, but you must also learn to scoop up that ground, put a handful in your pocket and carry your space in your heart.

Returning to my Easter sermon, I would compare this to the risen Jesus meeting the disciples as they were out fishing—or doing their daily work. In that sermon, I compare fishing to preaching,[15] in part because preaching is my work, the work I am doing right now, in fact! For you, let fishing symbolize *your* work, whatever calls you away from the place where you keep vigil.

In John's Gospel, the fisherman-disciples catch nothing all night long.[16] I think that you will share their experience when you leave your upper room and go outside your spiritual house to your own sea, where you are busy about many things: fishing for new accounts, for blockbuster projects, for big-catch clients, for the perfect dinner entree. I suspect you have angled for many such fish in your own sea, the waters of which lap loudly against your holy shore, sometimes eroding the banks of your holy ground. What is it that you are fishing for? How many hours do you spend with your nets dragging the water—sometimes coming up empty?

If fishing feels a far distance from your place of prayer, you need to become a spiritual camper, able to carry your home on your back or, more precisely, in the back of your heart.

How is this possible? For me, it was often a matter of memory. I had spent so much time in my cell that I could recall the very crispness of the air, the feel of the crevice where I supported my back, the hues of gray and brown that cocooned me in silence. I could go there when I was far away. You may call it pretense; I call it spiritual groundedness. The cave is as real as the lake. I can even fish from there, casting my net from the center of my being.

Remembering, then, is first. Second is halting your movement in space. While you may not be able to be in two *different* places at once, you can choose to be in one place that is portable, not unlike the space suits that your astronauts wear when they circle the earth. When I fish (preach), I wear my spiritual space suit. No matter where I am walking, I am wrapped in the wisdom acquired in the cave at Forli.

My third piece of advice may appear to contradict my earlier wisdom. For now, I must tell you to forget your cell, your cave, your place of prayer and be where you are—and in no other place. Be about your work, the demands of your world, of your day. Bring your whole self to serve wherever you are called.

I can say this with confidence because the self you bring is shaped by the place you call holy. It is like bringing the body which has exercised to sit at your desk. Even though you will not be exercising, the muscles which you have stretched and strengthened will support you in your new task, one in which you are exercising your mind more than your muscles.

This will happen—if you are spiritually in tune—much like gears shifting automatically in your car. You will choose what is best. You will be at home.

For Reflection

- **Pay Attention:** *List places which have stirred you spiritually: chapels where you have prayed or ancient places where your spiritual ancestors have worshipped; natural beauties such as oceans and mountains; rooms in your own home or in public buildings. Make a second list of "accessories" which assist you in your prayer: icons or other images, books or pictures, scents, colors, textures, music. Third, list peak moments of prayer and consider whether anything on your previous lists was present.*

- **Stake a Claim:** *Experiment. Use what you have learned in your earlier reflections to claim your own holy ground. Use photos of your holy places if they are far away. If they are nearby, consider returning to them frequently. Create a haven within your own home. Claim a corner or fill a spiritual treasure box with what you have experienced as helpful, even crucial, to your reflection.*

- **Keep Frequent Vigil:** *Practice. Persist in what moves you; discard what doesn't support you on your spiritual journey. Be faithful to what you have learned.*

- **Carry Your House in Your Heart:** *Imagine. When you are away from your spiritual supports, bring them to you through the power of your imagination. Act as if you are on your holy ground. Or, find your ground in the place where you are. Inventory the assets of this place and use them to root you in prayer.*

Closing Prayer

Use "Holy Ground" from the album *Be Exalted* by John Michael Talbot & Friends (The Sparrow Corporation, 1986). If the album is unavailable to you, the lyrics, which affirm the message of this day, follow:

This is holy ground. We're standing on holy ground. For the Lord is present and where [God] is, is holy!

These are holy hands. [God's] given us holy hands. [God] works through these hands and so these hands are holy!

Notes

[1] W. B. Yeats, "The Lake Isle of Innisfree," *The Poems* (New York: MacMillan Publishing Company, 1983), p. 39.

[2] Yeats, p. 39.

[3] See Marcil, p. 85.

[4] Genesis 26:2-3.

[5] *Life of St. Anthony*, p. 10.

[6] Marcil, p. 81.

[7] John 20:1.

[8] Matthew 28:6.

[9] Matthew 28:10.

[10] Matthew 28:5.

[11] Matthew 28:7.

[12] Annie Dillard, *Pilgrim at Tinker Creek* (New York: Bantam Books, Inc., 1974), p. 82.

[13] Marcil, p. 87.

[14] Dillard, p. 201.

[15] Marcil, p. 85.

[16] See John 21:6.

Franciscan Spiritual Center
6902 SE Lake Road Suite 300
Milwaukie, OR 97267-2148

DAY THREE
Finding Time

Coming Together in the Spirit

Fold this flower where you never forget.
Put me by where time no longer counts.
Then come back to a sure remembering....

—Carl Sandburg[1]

You have followed me like the people of my own day. I am amazed and humbled. In my own century, ordinary folks had no watches, no day-planners, no radios or televisions. If you are thinking that this means they had plenty of time, let me assure you that you have as much as they ever did.

Thirteenth-century women often spent the entire day laundering. Tradespeople could not telephone to set up appointments. I myself spent months walking from one town to another, traveling by foot from Italy to the south of France and back again over a period of three years.

"High loveliness hovers in time/ and is made of passing moments,"[2] writes Carl Sandburg, a poet of your own time. He suggests that you have to treasure time, preserving "high moments" like dried flower petals. It takes time even to remember where you have placed your own treasured petal, recalling your trace of grace. This is important, though, in developing strategies to steward time well.

Defining Our Thematic Context

I hope that you have already reclaimed your direction and a place of repose. Now, like Sandburg, you require "a sure remembering." You have already been "spending" time looking for what you have misplaced or misspent in your life.

I invite you to face in the direction you have discovered on Day One, rest in the place you have recovered on Day Two and reset your spiritual clock. The hands of your present-day timepiece can whirl, twirl, race and zoom. Or they can stand still. They can point upward in the traditional prayer position.

I want to search with you for time. Before you can find this elusive gift, though, you need to remember how it looks and feels. We want to find "high moments." I want you to not only have time but also to treasure it as an opportunity for "sure remembering."

Opening Prayer

Here I am, Lord!
Help me to stay.
Still the ticking
of my heart clock,
my mind chimes,
my footfalls.

Stay, still, stop,
my soul.
Be seated,
be slowed,
be silent,
be soft.

Here I am, Lord!
I set my watch
to keep watch
with you.

I wait upon your word.
I will be filled
and my heart will rejoice.
I will know the time
and I will keep it.

Retreat Session Three
Slide-bolt Your Time With Love

I suspect that, in your search for time, you will not be satisfied with simple sufficiency. You will be hard to please here! You don't want the time to hang heavy. Neither do you want it to fly. You will want to be free of demands on your time, yet you will demand much of the time you discover.

What you want is more time than other people have. What you want is more freedom, more discretion with the gift of time than other people have. I have a reputation as a wonder-worker, but I can neither extend the hours of your day nor empty it of distractions.

In my *Sermones*, which are actually sermon notes to share with others who preach God's Word, I wrote these comments on Jesus' appearance to his disciples in the upper room after his Resurrection: "A person sanctifies the sabbath day when that person remains in peace of spirit and keeps himself or herself from illicit works.... The [locked] doors are the five senses of the body, which we must close with the slide-bolt of love...."[3]

I believe that it is not so much actual hours of daylight or work time or solitude of which you feel deprived. For myself, it was the absence of God which I felt most keenly. This absence had opposite effects: It could make every hour seem a week of mourning or it could make time race—with me running after to hold its shirttail, seeing life in a blur.

This first-described time is the experience of the disciples in the upper room. They believe they should be about the Father's business, but all they can do is puzzle, pace and second-guess themselves. They are not thinking about Jesus but about themselves. This is spiritual slow time.

Fast time is equally unreflective: It is the hurry of the disciples casting nets out again and again, unthinking, desperate, exhausted.[4] Time stops and your spiritual timepieces are synchronized only when you take time to inquire, "Who are you?"[5] and when you know in whose presence you are, to pray "You know that I love you."[6]

I do not wish you to think this easy: this time-finding, this time-keeping. It was a struggle for me even when it seemed it should be easy. In my early years as an Augustinian, I lived at Sao Vicente de Fora, supposedly secure from the bustle of Lisbon's merchants, traders and traffic. But this did not guarantee me the time I judged sufficient to be a man of God. So what is this time I sought if I could not find it there in so apparently suitable a place?

It is to be aware of the time all the time—and mysteriously outside time's constraints as well. It is to know that *now* is the time, "time to seek the LORD, that he may come and rain righteousness upon you."[7] It is the time Paul described, "See, now is the acceptable time; see, now is the day of salvation!"[8] It is to know that *now* is also *always* because you are to remain ever in this now.

Let me suggest an image to you. When I preached on the wedding feast at Cana, I suggested that the six stone jars had a moral interpretation: six ways to purify the soul.[9] Today, I want to offer yet another moral interpretation. Today I see the six jars as testimony to the hope that Jesus' "hour" will come: His time and our time will converge. We, too, will have reason for a feast!

Each jar is one part of that faithful filling of yourself so that the Lord will come to reveal his glory poured out in you. Fix your eyes and your mind on each jar in turn so that the eternal God can reveal the now-time bubbling up in you.

The First Stone Jar: Time to Breathe

I am called a Doctor of the Church, an Evangelical Doctor. It is my learning and wisdom, particularly gained from the Scriptures, that has brought me this honor. Nonetheless, my "doctoring" has often been of the body as well as of the mind and the soul.

Doctors of my day held a mirror to the mouth, checking for evidence of breathing on that surface. Breathing can be evidence of spiritual health as well. Hold the mirror up to yourself.

In your common conversation, you complain, "I don't have time to breathe" and sigh, "I need to take a breather." Take a breath. Drink from the first stone jar now. Simply breathe.

Attend to your breathing. When you breathe in, picture it as taking in to yourself the power of the universe, which you filter through the miracle of your respiration. You release what is not needed for your life and health. Breathe in. Breathe out.

You may prefer to focus only on the physical act

which your Creator has empowered you to perform. Or you may wish a word-prayer of two syllables: one for the in-breath and one for its release. To me, this seems very near to the directions you are given for the aerobic exercise so popular in your century. (Much aerobic activity was required of us who lived in the twelfth and thirteenth century, though we did not know your modern terms for it!) The word *aerobic* simply means *with oxygen*. That is also how you are to exercise your spirit—by filling your first stone jar with oxygen, by taking time to breathe!

The Second Stone Jar: Time to Pare Away

The six stone jars—before they contained excellent wine for the wedding guests—were filled with water for traditional ceremonial washing. This symbolic washing is not so different from the baptismal reminder we give ourselves with holy water as we enter a church. This second jar, the jar of release, is a second aspect of finding time. It, too, represents cleansing, a letting go in the dimension of time.

A practice I learned in the monastery was the particular examen. I offer it to you as a time-finder. Examine your use of time. Write in a notebook how you have used the time you have been so graciously given. Express your thanks for this gift. Ask God's forgiveness when you squander it. Ask God's help in using time in ways that honor the hours that are yours.

I ask you not to abandon times of reverie and delight. These are not time wasted, but the very moments in which I myself found the grace of God warming me like a sunbeam piercing the clouds of distraction and chaos. Unless you pare away time spent in worry and rushing, or in the modern pastimes of shopping and watching TV, you will never notice the clouds parting. This second jar can be filled with sunbeams if you will allow the time.

The Third Stone Jar: Time to Be Silent

Just as the jars of Cana were all filled with water from the same source, these six stone jars represent all the time you have. Yet each jar is also distinct just as you are able to mark off the seconds, minutes and hours of your time and schedule them to be used in various ways.

I say this to you because as you take time to breathe, to pare away distractions and simplify your days, you will also drink from the water jar of silence and find in it good spirits. My life reveals a search for the silence that renews, for time in which such silence can settle in the soul. I once wrote, "The contemplative person goes off alone, keeping far away from the restless throng...seeking solitude for body and soul."[10]

You may need to drink from this jar by rising earlier or keeping a vigil late into a quiet evening. You may claim time for silence by walking alone in midday or after the evening meal. You may need to speak aloud your need for a time without speech. It is not a common request in your day though it is a common need.

In Brive, France, where I founded a new Franciscan house in 1126, I remained for some time. I required there a little shelter in a grotto near the friary. Here I found time to be silent. Today the people of Brive point to a fountain I made to catch water coming from the rocks.[11] I prefer you to see that in Brive I filled the stone jar of silence.

The Fourth Stone Jar: Time to Remember

When you find time for silence, you will soon discover that the emptiness is quickly filled with sound. It is like the situation Matthew describes, "When the unclean spirit has gone out of a person, it wanders through waterless regions looking for a resting place, but it finds none. Then it says, 'I will return to my house from which I came.' When it comes, it finds it empty, swept, and put in order. Then it goes and brings along seven other spirits more evil than itself, and they enter and live there."[12]

This may be interpreted as the soul emptying itself of noise, but leaving the heart unoccupied, which leaves room for louder noises still to come in and settle! So, my friends, give your silence to remembering.

I do not mean that you are to remember the groceries to be bought, the overdue library books to be returned, the checkbook to be balanced or the grass to be mowed. I mean Sandburg's "sure remembering." This is what he is describing when he writes, "I have kept high moments. They go round and round in me." From the fourth stone jar, you are to draw such moments, moments such as Mary held in her heart.[13]

What moments do I encourage you to draw out, to pour upon your memory? Remember when you have experienced the presence of God. Remember when you have seen God incarnated on the streets of your city, in your home, in your husband or wife, in your children. Remember when you have seen God in the splendors of creation.

I have heard your popular song, "Try to Remember." The song concludes, "And if you remember, follow."[14] Yes, yes, all this time-finding is one treasure, divided for now into six stone jars. As you remember, you will want to know what the blessing of the memory is for you. When you have drunk of memory, you must listen to its lessons.

The Fifth Stone Jar: Time to Listen

I who was so often a preacher required time to listen so that I might preach what I had heard. When you have heard—when God's many gifts to you have bubbled up and poured over into your memory, you must listen for their meaning, for their gift to you in this time of your life.

This is the fermenting, the percolating, the rising of memory into inspiration. This is its blessing. It is not enough to remember—you must follow. You must follow the memory into meaning.

Many people reflect on the life of Jesus, on my life and the life of other saints to learn what they must do. This can certainly be part of your remembering and listening. If you are to find time—and that is the search that is taking us from stone jar to stone jar today—you also need to bring your own life into focus alongside these exemplary life journeys. You need to experience a "tesseract" or "wrinkle in time."

Madeleine L'Engle, a wise twentieth-century writer, described tesseracts in her book *A Wrinkle in Time*. Tesseracts, or time-wrinkles, are journeys into the fifth dimension, beyond present time and space.[15] You need to experience a time-wrinkle yourself. You can truly find time, blessed eternal time, by experiencing Jesus, yourself and your potential all in one fifth-dimensional moment. That is how I can know Carl Sandburg, Annie Dillard and Madeleine L'Engle, even though they live in other times and spaces. That is how you can know Jesus and let him lead you into the next moment of grace.

Wrinkles in time take no time (in the first four dimensions). Drinking from these first five stone jars can bring you to find time where you thought there was none. You have all the time you need. You have all the richness of the past and all the power of the future. You have reason to rejoice.

The Sixth Stone Jar: Time to Rejoice

"If the spiritual person lays aside the cares and distractions of this life, if this person enters into the house of conscience and closes the door of the senses, then that soul finds peace in wisdom, because he or she gives the self over to the contemplation of heavenly things and tastes the quiet of celestial delights."[16] This is what happens when you find time, when you claim the time that is yours, when you use it to breathe, to pare away, to be silent, to listen and to remember. To do this, you have to close the door, to bolt it with the "slide-bolt of love."

Can you do this? I promise you that moments of connection with the Almighty and All-merciful will fall into your lap, pressed down, shaken together and running over, "for the measure you give will be the measure you get back."[17] That measure is your spiritual timepiece, your holy hourglass.

The sixth stone jar, then, will fill your cup of rejoicing, your cup of alleluias, your own cup of celestial delights. Take this time in great and grateful gulps. You are not to check off some spiritual obligation to pray and then fail to sip the final brew of the wedding feast, the cup of rejoicing.

In my own life, this time is symbolized in all the images you see of me holding the Infant Jesus. Holding a baby, delighting in the miracle of infancy—wriggling, lively, bouncing—this is the very essence of joy. I will not settle for you here whether it is the stuff of legend or history, but it is certainly the stuff of parable and metaphor. I like Madeleine Pecora Nugent's account of the story, because she makes of the infant a laughing,

happy baby and of myself a playful guardian.[18]
This is the true miracle when you find time for the deep truths of life: You will see Jesus. Jesus will delight in you. You will drink from the sixth stone jar. It is a cup of happiness. You will not need to unlock the door of the inner/upper room. You will be able to walk through it!

For Reflection

Drink from each of the stone jars:

- **Breathe:** *Whenever you look at your watch, let that glance serve as a reminder to breathe in and out slowly, using words or syllables which help you to center yourself.*

- **Pare Away:** *Decide on two times during the day/evening for an examination of how you have spent your time. Ask yourself: Which moments were best spent? Which may have been ill-spent?*

- **Be Silent:** *Where will you make a space for silence in your day? How will you ensure that it can happen?*

- **Remember:** *Play or sing the song, "Try to Remember." Use it as a prayer. Pray through a family album. As you look at each photo, remember the blessings of the occasion which you chose to photograph and place in your album of memories.*

- **Listen:** *Find a copy of Madeleine L'Engle's* A Wrinkle in Time. *The entire book can easily be a message concerning your own wrestling with time. If you already know the book, simply reread the final chapter, "The Foolish and the Weak." Experience a time-wrinkle with Meg Murry, Charles Wallace, IT and yourself.*

■ **Rejoice:** *Do something childlike to celebrate all the time you have been given. Eat cotton candy. Swing. Play in the snow. Shout exuberantly! Pick dandelions and place them before a statue of the Infant Jesus.*

Closing Prayer

Let us humbly implore God, my dearest sisters
   and brothers,
that we may be allowed to celebrate
the wedding feast in Cana of Galilee,
to fill up the six stone jars with water,
in order that we may merit to drink
the wine of eternal joy with Jesus
at the wedding feast of the eternal Jerusalem,
who is blessed, praiseworthy, and glorious
through eternal ages.
May every soul, bride of the Holy Spirit,
say, "Amen. Alleluia."

—Prayer of Saint Anthony[19]

Notes

[1] Carl Sandburg, "High Moments," *Honey and Salt* (New York: Harcourt Brace Jovanovich, 1963), p. 68.

[2] Sandburg, p. 68.

[3] Marcil, p. 93.

[4] See John 21.

[5] John 21:12.

[6] John 21:17.

[7] Hosea 10:12b.

[8] 2 Corinthians 6:2b.

[9] Jarmak, p. 107.

[10] Clasen, p. 21.

[11] Clasen, p. 79.

[12] Matthew 12:43-45.

[13] See Luke 2:51.

[14] Tom Jones and Harvey Schmidt, *The Fantasticks* (New York: Applause Theatre Book Publishers, 1990), p. 35.

[15] Madeleine L'Engle, *A Wrinkle in Time* (New York: Farrar, Straus and Giroux, 1962).

[16] Clasen, p. 83.

[17] Luke 6:38.

[18] Madeline Pecora Nugent, *Praying With Anthony of Padua* (Winona, Minn.: Saint Mary's Press, 1996), pp. 184-185.

[19] Jarmak, p. 109.

DAY FOUR
Finding Balance

Coming Together in the Spirit

Humans are amphibians—half spirit and half animal.... As spirits they belong to the eternal world, but as animals they inhabit time. This means that while their spirit can be directed to an eternal object, their bodies, passions, and imaginations are in continual change, for to be in time means to change. Their nearest approach to constancy, therefore, is undulation—the repeated return to a level from which they repeatedly fall back, a series of troughs and peaks.

—C. S. Lewis[1]

Defining Our Thematic Context

In C. S. Lewis's *The Screwtape Letters*, which is an anthology of imaginary letters from Uncle Screwtape—an Under Secretary to Satan—to his nephew and novice tempter Wormwood, Screwtape encourages Wormwood to capitalize on the "troughs" and "peaks" of humans, "to make good use" of human undulation.

For me, coming to know Francis of Assisi was crucial to achieving balance in my own life. Francis sensed that I struggled with the balance between learning and loving, between scholarship and spiritual expression.

He penned a fatherly note to me, saying, "It is agreeable to me that you should teach the friars sacred theology, so long as they do not extinguish the spirit of prayer and devotedness over this study."[2]

Heresy, I think, is often a question of balance. The word itself, from the Greek *hairein*, meaning "to take," suggests a dangerous tipping or "taking away" such a balance.

I spent nine years of my life preaching in Italy and France, gaining, I am embarrassed to tell you, the reputation of being "the hammer of heretics."[3] My hope was not to hammer any person, but to restore spiritual balance by hammering home the truth as I understood it from Scripture and other sources of wisdom. I want to consider with you some imbalances that tempted our age and invite you to ponder those that tempt yours.

Opening Prayer

I reach out to you,
O Lord of leaps and bounds,
but I teeter,
I tremble,
I sway on the edge
of awareness.

I have learned of you.
I have met you.
I have known you.
I have loved you.

You wait for me
beneath the trapeze.
You hold the net of safety
in your strong and faithful hands.

You hold me up
when I fear to fall.
You hold me down
when I seem to float.
You stretch me taut
when I shrivel small.
You hug me close
when I fall apart.

You are mighty God.
I can fall
only into your arms.

RETREAT SESSION FOUR
In the Middle of Every Heart

Each person's center of gravity, the place where he or
she is in tune with the universe, balanced and serene, is
different. Musical harmonies shift from chord to chord.
The same note cannot be sustained indefinitely. Spiritual
balance is unique to each person and varies throughout
the days of a person's life. Yes, we undulate. We are not
all asked to balance on one toe like a ballerina or strike a
perilous pose on the circus trapeze. Yet the same
confidence, the same courage, the same inward grace is
required.

"'I am among you as one who serves.'[4] [Jesus] stands
in the middle in every heart; he stands in the middle so
that from him, as from a center, all the lines of grace
might stretch outward to us who are at the circumference,
revolving and moving about him."[5]

I can testify to this mighty power—these lines of

blessed grace—at work throughout my life, but wish now to focus especially on my preaching missions in France and Italy. There, my challenge was to strengthen people of faith to face the temptation to lean too far to the left or the right, even to fall from balance, to move from the middle of their hearts.

I am suggesting three such tightropes which faced us in medieval times. You may find that you have teetered on these ropes yourself. And I say to you, "Stay 'in the middle,' therefore, and you will have peace with your neighbor. If you do not stay in the middle, you will not be able to have peace...."[6]

Between Word and Work

The first undulation I wish to address is between word and work. Your modern musical, *My Fair Lady*,[7] includes a song called "Show Me." Eliza Doolittle, a woman of humble origins, (perhaps her accent is something like the Portuguese edge on my Italian) sings, "Words! Words! Words! I'm so sick of words!... If you're in love, show me!"[8] Eliza certainly didn't want or expect total silence but rather a balance and harmony between what was said and what was done.

Eliza's admirer Freddy was plying her with more of the aristocratic mumbo-jumbo that was supposed to be making such a difference in her life, but it appeared to be all talk. Eliza wanted a hug, a kiss—some evidence of Freddy's affections. "Never do I ever want to hear another word. There isn't one I haven't heard,"[9] she complains.

Toward the end of the twelfth century, the Waldensians, who sought to be poor like the poor Christ, took scandal at the behavior of the clergy, that is, the behavior of my fellow priests. The Waldensians had raised a tune much like Eliza Doolittle's, saying, "Don't just preach the good word. Live it." They began with a straightforward challenge which the Church would have done well to acknowledge and address. Eventually, though, they severed their connection with the Church to express their contempt for ordination and for the Mass.

This was not the main heresy I was asked to counter with my preaching. Still I met many people who were thrown off balance by its assertions, just as these Poor of Lyon, followers of the French Valdes (also written as *Waldes*), were confused by hypocrisy in their priests. As I preached, "When merely the mouth of the preacher and not his life speaks, no fountain of water can come forth from the rocky ground. The face of the preacher is his way of acting, for in it is reflected his true countenance. This face must shine like the sun, that in our works all may see what we have learned by faith."[10]

So you can see that I *urged* priests to make their words one with their lives. I asked the same of myself and I ask it now of you who also preach a powerful message by your lives. I know it is difficult. Your words can run ahead of you. You may say what you wish was true, hoping to catch up to your words. Or you may say what you think will please someone or inspire a listener, even if you aren't able to act on it yourself. You confuse and contradict yourself. You can spread confusion among others.

So, are you to keep silence then? No, I simply ask you to speak the truth. Will you do it always? Knowing people as I do, I think not. But, you can begin first by attending more to the gaps between your own words and actions rather than to those of others. "First take the log out of your own eye"[11] or, should I say, from your own mouth.

Second, you can soften your assertions, not of eternal

truth, but of personal opinion and observation. You do not need to state your own opinions as though they have the force of law. In truth, you would do well to remember that they seldom carry such weight.

Third, you can remember that "[T]ongues, they will cease; as for knowledge, it will come to an end. For we know only in part, and we prophesy only in part; but when the complete comes, the partial will come to an end."[12] Words are not always necessary. I once heard the wisdom, "Speak only if you can improve on the silence." That might be too drastic a measure to imagine, but I'm sure you catch its spirit.

Perhaps you do not lean so much toward words. You teeter more toward impetuous action. It is not your mouth but your hands and feet that trip you up. I faced this challenge. I knew that people *might* listen to me, but could be *counted* upon to watch my actions. I once said, "The difference between saying and doing is as great as was that between creating and re-creating. Creation, in a sense, was simple and easy, for it was done by word alone, or rather by God's will alone, for God's willing is his speaking. Re-creation, however, was extremely difficult because it was done by suffering and dying.[13] It is this "suffering and dying" that people will expect to see in you if you are walking at all the tightrope of word and work.

Just to offer one example: Are you living and working in complete comfort? At whose cost? People walked days to hear me preach and in such numbers that I often spoke outdoors. I did not insist on pulpit or shade. I spoke in my clearest, strongest voice, teaching them the word of God and its challenges, encouraging them to be faithful, and I stayed to hear their confessions late into the night. I took no time for lunch, though people picnicked all around me. (What was I to say? "For your penance, please offer a few of those grapes to your confessor"?) I did not want to keep people waiting. I loved them too much.

I would also urge people not to judge by appearances, but it is a great temptation. In considering your undulations, you do well to consider a balance between appearances and inward realities. Do they speak in concert or discord?

Do not look to my life, however—or to the lives of others—but your own. Bring your words and your work to the center and there you will find Christ who will hold you up as you find the balance.

Between Body and Soul

"Amphibians," C. S. Lewis says of us. Spirit, yes, but "bodies, passions, and imaginations" as well. We live in the land of physicality, but we thirst for the waters of spirit. For three years, my mission in France was to offer refreshment to the thirsty of soul but to announce also the mystery of the Incarnation. In tracing the story of Jesus from the heavens to the earth on which we walk, I wanted the people of Carcassonne, Toulouse, Albi, Agen and Razès to long to be like Jesus, who chose a body while honoring the soul. He expressed the struggle well: "The spirit indeed is willing, but the flesh is weak."[14] It is a question of balance.

My friends, the Cathari (from the Greek word for "pure"), struggled to understand this tension between body and soul. They concluded that good is spiritual and evil is material—and vice versa. Theirs is an appealing romantic spirit, also traceable in the troubadours and the courtly love tradition of bodiless affection. Some legends say that the Cathars guarded the Holy Grail, whose earlier keepers lacked the purity to protect the treasure.

It's possible that the Cathari emphasis on soul was a countermeasure against over-attention to the body, especially among those who were expected to show us the truth of the gospel. They went too far, which is the harm of heresy, a good point taken beyond its merit.

Franciscan Father Lothar Hardick explains the Cathari thinking well: "[The Cathari] held the view that all material, earthly reality was fundamentally corrupt and evil because it was created by an evil god. It was particularly in sexual production of life that they saw the real sin. Anyone who desired to be 'pure' would have to avoid all contact with anything that came into existence through sexual procreation.... The Cathari rejected all sacraments since these involved material things: bread, wine, oil, etc. And since, in their view, it was inconceivable that the spiritual nature of the Word could have united itself with an earthly body, they denied that Christ had been truly human. The Redeemer had assumed only an apparent body; his sufferings had been only apparent and not real."[15]

Thinking of this sort created a near resignation to evil among the Cathari of Southern France. If their lay preachers had spoken the truth, they were conceived in sin, their beautiful children were the offspring of sin, they were in constant need of food, warmth and love only because they were bodily sinners. And Jesus had *not* been like them "in all things but sin." Jesus was a stranger to their humanity.

Are the Cathari so far from you and your struggle to believe in God, to believe in Jesus, to believe that you are good, body and soul? Today, I feel certain that some of you think your body evil and your soul in danger. I say to you what I preached on the feast of the Exaltation of the Holy Cross, "'Your life [body and soul] hangs before you' on the Cross so that you might see yourself as in a mirror,

examining and scrutinizing yourself in it.... If you pause
to reflect profoundly, you will realize how sublime is your
dignity, and how excellent your worth, which demanded
so high a price. You cannot better appreciate your worth
than by looking into the mirror of the Cross of Christ."[16]
Look again in this mirror. Try to imagine yourself as
soul alone. Examine yourself. Saint Paul says to you,
"[D]o you not know that your bodies are members of
Christ?"[17] and "[D]o you not know that your body is a
temple of the Holy Spirit?"[18]

See your reflection in the mirror. Is it a body only
whose eyes look back at you? Is it your body to which
you are attending in this retreat? Is your body asking for
attention now? Do you need to grant its every demand?
Can you deny its every wish? The heresy of today is, as it
was in medieval times, to remain at either end of the
tightrope—body or soul—rather than to attempt a
marvelous balance and to live with the undulation.

Between Judgment and Compassion

Those the Church called heretics judged the Church
wanting and had no compassion for the human weakness
of its members. In turn, the Church often judged them
harshly as well, failing to grant them a hearing or to
acknowledge the flaws of the orthodox.

My preaching mission to France was not, however, a
visitation of judgment. I sometimes spoke harshly of the
clergy, I admit, but not of the people, the crowds. For
them, I preached with love, probing every word of
Scripture for messages to move their minds and hearts.

When they had heard the word of God's love for
them, I offered to demonstrate the forgiveness of God
through sacramental confession. I prayed, "Let us ask the
Lord Jesus Christ, who is Son of the compassionate

Father, to fill us with His mercy, that we may show compassion to ourselves and to others; that we may judge no one, that we may not condemn anyone...."[19]

The role of a judge is to apply the law, to decide, to criticize or censure. In his memoir of childhood, Frank McCourt remembers much of censure and repression. I am glad that he also remembers a fellow Franciscan as a compassionate advocate, expressing sympathy, tenderness and clemency.

McCourt recounts his confession on his sixteenth birthday: "I did terrible things," he tells Friar Gregory. The friar responds, "God forgives all who repent. He sent His only Beloved Son to die for us." And Frank McCourt is moved to tell the kind friar a host of troubles—some sins of his own, some the sins of others, some simply the way of things in Limerick.

> Father Gregory says, Would you like to sit and be silent, perhaps pray a few minutes?
> His brown robe is rough against my cheek and there's a smell of soap. He looks at St. Francis and the tabernacle and nods and I suppose he's talking to God. Then he tells me kneel, gives me absolution, tells me say three Hail Marys, three Our Fathers, three Glory Bes. He tells me God forgives me and I must forgive myself, that God loves me and I must love myself for only when you love God in yourself can you love all God's creatures."[20]

When I knew someone as Father Gregory knew young Frank, I always hoped to express God's compassion as well as God's judgment—which may indeed be one and the same. This was my sacramental calling—to express the balance. I, in turn, call you.

I believe that the balance here is in the conscious decision to be compassionate. In this retreat, I speak of Father Gregory, but I add your name as well. Why? I see even more clearly that the forgiveness expressed by the confessor needs to be evident in your attitude and in your actions. In this way, you demonstrate that your debt has been lifted and you give hope to the rest. You see their debts, but you forgive them. Each one expresses this to the next and together you will dare to approach the seat of judgment.

To speak as our Father Francis wrote to me, it is agreeable to me that you speak, but be careful that your work expresses the Word as well. It is agreeable to me that you prize your soul, but take care to honor the created world in which you have been placed. Do not allow the light that is there to be extinguished. And, lastly, see clearly yet forgive generously. In the peaks and troughs of these undulations, you will ride the wave, finding the middle, a place in God's heart.

For Reflection

■ *Consider your personal heresies. What are your own spiritual imbalances? When have you teetered toward the edge of excess? When have you failed in generosity?*

■ *Consider the heresies, tensions or imbalances of the age. What words might collectively describe them for you— consumerism, prejudice, isolation, despair, pride? Others? Did Jesus speak to these tensions in parable? Do you have your own parable, a story which expresses the difficulty of finding the middle ground?*

■ *In each of the three tensions named in this session, where do you find yourself? Which way do you lean? What can you do to achieve balance?*

Closing Prayer

Let us therefore pray to our Lord Jesus Christ
that he give us the grace to seek his Kingdom
and to build within ourselves a moral Jerusalem.
By doing this,
we will be able to merit our place
    in the heavenly Jerusalem
to sing Alleluia in its streets
with all the saints and angels.
But the One whose Kingdom is eternal for all ages
must help us to do so.

—*Prayer of Saint Anthony*[21]

Notes

[1] C. S. Lewis, *The Screwtape Letters* (New York: Bantam Books, 1982), p. 22.

[2] "Letter to St. Anthony," Marion Habig, ed., *St. Francis of Assisi: Writings and Early Biographies* (Quincy, Ill.: Franciscan Press, 1991), p. 164.

[3] Clasen, p. 70.

[4] Luke 22:27.

[5] Marcil, p. 95-96.

[6] Marcil, p. 96.

[7] Alan Jay Lerner and Frederick Lowe, *My Fair Lady: A Musical Play in Two Acts* (New York: Coward-McCann, Inc., 1956).

[8] Lerner and Lowe, p. 146.

[9] Lerner and Lowe, p. 146.

[10] Clasen, p. 72.

[11] Matthew 7:5.

[12] 1 Corinthians 13:9-10.

[13] Marcil, p. 167.

[14] Matthew 26:41.

[15] Father Lothar Hardick, O.F.M., trans. Father Zachary Hayes, O.F.M., and Father Jason M. Miskuly, O.F.M., *Anthony of Padua:*

Proclaimer of the Gospel (Strasbourg, France: Editions du Signe, 1994), p. 16.

[16] Jarmak, p. 144.

[17] 1 Corinthians 6:15.

[18] 1 Corinthians 6:19.

[19] Jarmak, pp. 33-34.

[20] Frank McCourt, *Angela's Ashes* (London: HarperCollins, 1996), p. 403.

[21] Fr. Livio Poloniato, O.F.M. Conv., ed., *Seek First His Kingdom: An Anthology of the Sermons of the Saint* (Padua, Italy: Conventual Franciscan Friars, 1988), p. 121.

DAY FIVE
Finding the Right Words

Coming Together in the Spirit

> *A word is dead*
> *When it is said,*
> *Some say.*
> *I say it just*
> *Begins to live*
> *That day.*
>   —Emily Dickinson[1]

Defining Our Thematic Context

God gave me many opportunities to speak the living word. You know of my travels in southern France and Italy to preach the word. I continued to preach until the last months of my life. My first biographer described my work in a way that pleases me: "[G]oing about cities and castles, villages and countrysides, he sowed the seed of life most abundantly and fervently."[2] The evangelist Luke says, "The seed is the word of God."[3] I am not here to make preachers of you, but I do wish that you be planters of the word. The words that you say must lead others to God.

The words that I preached and wrote were

strengthened by much reading, not only of Scripture but also of many other sources. I read Aristotle, Cicero and Augustine as well as the writings of many other saints. I read natural history, the history of nations, the history of words. I used these words to understand God's "all-powerful word [which] leaped from heaven, from the royal throne."[4] I wish to call attention to your reading and the ways in which it shapes your thought, your speaking and your writing.

Your contemporary author Ernest Hemingway wrote a letter in which he said, "All my life I've looked at words as though I were seeing them for the first time."[5] I want you to see words again and let it be as the first time. Let us pray to find vision.

Opening Prayer

Jesus,
you are the word made flesh,
the almighty word from heaven,
the word of life.

May I hear only your word.
May I speak only your word.
May my very flesh be shaped
by the word of God.

I wish to listen with respect,
to speak with reverence and relish
the words of truth and compassion.

Give me now your word to hear
so that I may know that word to speak.

Retreat Session Five
The Word Is in God's Presence

Emily Dickinson's poem expresses her belief that the spoken word is alive. In my time, giving your word was a binding contract. I know your times are more complicated and require signatures on legal papers. Yet even those are words upon words.

Words have the power to bind and to sever, to inspire and to dishearten, to make peace and to cause war. When I look at the story of creation in Genesis, I see that God the Creator spoke powerful words that shaped the world. This same power of the word is expressed in the prologue of John's Gospel: "In the beginning was the Word: the Word was with God, and the Word was God. ...[T]he Word became flesh and lived among us, and we have seen his glory."[6]

I have seen this glory myself. When I preached at the ordinations at Forli, without a moment to prepare my message, I myself was amazed at how the friars responded to my message. No biographer recorded my text from that day, but my first biographer says that I was the "reed of the Holy Spirit."[7] This I believe—and I remember it now so that I can urge you, too, to be a reed. A spiritual writer of your century, Caryll Houselander, praised Mary with similar words: "She [Mary] was a reed through which the Eternal Love was to be piped as a shepherd's song."[8]

Houselander says of Mary that she makes it possible for humans to see that God is connected with our ordinariness, our humanity. Mary, she said, gave a human voice to God. As must we.

The Word That Is Said

In my sermon notes, I identified "five words with meaning."[9] Saint Paul has written, "I would rather speak five words with my mind, in order to instruct others also, than ten thousand words in a tongue."[10] I believe these five words that Paul wanted to speak are "the word of prayer, the word of praise, the word of counsel, the word of encouragement, and word of confession."[11] I tried to speak these five words in my century and believe they are the right words to include in your spiritual vocabulary today. They are words that bring life.

1. *The word of prayer*. This first word is a word of witness, words audible to others, words that demonstrate your faith. Consider not only promising to pray for others, but also praying with them at the moment you learn their need. This is the example of Jesus, who did not say to those in need of healing, "I will remember you in my prayers tonight."

Jesus' word was immediate. Jesus' word was loving. Jesus' word healed. Others hearing your prayer to God will be reassured that the line is open.

2. *The word of praise*. "Praised be Jesus Christ" was once a customary greeting among people of faith. Giving the glory to God for the presence of another person is surely a word of praise.

Praise directed to other persons is also praise of their Creator. To speak such words of praise, you will need to look for reasons everywhere—reasons to say, "You are so pleasant to be with," "You are a valuable contributor," "You are such a good neighbor" or "You are quite wise, you know!" In the same letter in which I found Paul's mention of the five intelligible words, he also praises the Corinthians: "In every way you have been enriched in him, in speech and knowledge of every kind" and "not lack[ing] in any spiritual gift."[12] Be generous with your praise, as Paul was.

3. The word of counsel. In your time, "counsel" seems to require a certificate or a diploma or a talk show. This has made counsel both expensive and cheap. The word of counsel, to be wise, needs to come from your own prayer and *after* it. This ensures that you are a "reed," speaking the truth as best human beings can.

Counsel is one of the gifts of the Holy Spirit. Waiting until you are asked for advice may ensure that your words find a home in the heart of the other.

4. The word of encouragement. I once heard that the human heart requires ten words of encouragement for every single word of criticism. While praise is a word offered for what is already good, encouragement is a word to strengthen and stiffen what needs more starch. Speak words like, "You are making great progress," "I can see a difference already" or "That was a step in the right direction."

Encourage surely means "to give courage." To encourage is to give people medals of honor (most often figuratively), just as the Wizard of Oz literally awarded them to the cowardly lion.

5. The word of confession. The last word I invite you to pronounce aloud is a word of sorrow. This may require courage as well as prayer. I mean this word on two levels, which are tightly linked. "[G]o; first be reconciled [make peace with] to your brother or sister, and then come and offer your gift."[13] Express your apologies as they are appropriate. Make up with people. This is a powerful word, though one sometimes hard to speak.

This word then naturally leads you also to celebrate the Sacrament of Reconciliation. I delighted in pronouncing absolution or forgiveness from sin. I spent hours after my sermons hearing the confessions of those moved by grace through my words. I hoped to inspire this response. As one biographer has noticed, "it would be hard to find a page in Anthony's *Sermones* where sacramental penance is not mentioned."[14] This was—and is—a special ministry of the Franciscan friars, this expression of the forgiveness of God and of the Church.

Your word of confession will be completed by God's word of forgiveness. These are the five words to be said and God's most singular word in response. "Put away from you all bitterness and wrath and anger and wrangling and slander, together with all malice, and be kind to one another, tenderhearted, forgiving one another, as God in Christ has forgiven you."[15]

The Word That Is Written by Others

Much that I know of prayer, praise, counsel, encouragement and confession I learned from holy books. One of the treasures I left behind when I joined the friars was the great library at the Coimbra monastery. There I had learned the approach to study espoused by the Canons of St. Victor, known as the Victorines. It began with reading, *lectio*, and concluded with preaching, *predicatio*. The word I had read, I broke open for the people. I then wrote that word down for others. Reading, then, was the first way in which I honored the written word.

For me, being taught by learned and holy men such as Don Peter Pires at Sao Vicente in Lisbon and Master John at Santa Cruz in Coimbra, was akin to reading. I saw how steeped they were in learning and I instinctively turned to their sources. I studied the Scriptures day and night and also read learned commentators.

Today, you have many other ways to learn in your multi-media environment. I would have enjoyed television's Discovery Channel, the Learning Channel and the many avenues on the Internet, although they are more difficult to take up and put down than books. Your century, too, is hungry for knowledge.

This reverie about my own sources of learning is simply to praise knowledge as a way toward God. Spiritual knowledge is primary, but it need not be separate from so-called secular subjects. Read the Bible, but also read the Book of the Universe.

I invite you, then, to share my hunger for words, by which I mean knowledge. When you learn how things work, praise God. When you see how great buildings are marvelously constructed, praise God. When you visit a zoo, an aquarium or a museum, praise God. I caution you, as Francis cautioned me, to be sure that the words and knowledge don't get in the way, but lead you to the Word.

The Word That Is Written by You

I listened to what I had learned and what I had said and I wrote it down in my sermon notes for Sundays and also in the feast day sermon notes which I did not live to complete. Do I hear you say you are not planning to write any books of your own?

Pens, pencils and computer terminals can be extensions of God's message. How many more people I might have reached if I had the avenues that are available to you!

It is your own heart that your written words will reach first. I learned that writing my thoughts slowed them, invited me to make connections between them, led me to stop in amazement at the confluences and congruences of my thought. I first wrote to myself and for myself. Your written words create a record for your own reference and reflection.

What might you write? You might keep a spiritual journal. You might correspond seriously with a friend, a mentor, a parent. You might record your "intelligible words" of prayer, praise, counsel, encouragement and even confession. Some of them might be shared with others. Words of encouragement are often treasured by others. Some of your words will be for yourself alone.

Holy Father Francis wrote a letter to the friars in which he urged all to care for the "liturgical books and anything else which contains [God's] holy words with great care. I urge all my friars and I encourage them in Christ to show all possible respect for God's words wherever they may happen to find them in writing. If they are not kept properly or if they lie thrown about disrespectfully, they should pick them up and put them aside, paying honor in his words to God who spoke them."[16]

I believe that the words of your life, intelligible and in tongues you have yet to understand, are all the word of God to you. Some words are scrambled still. Some are riddles and some are greater puzzles than that! But the codes can be deciphered—I give you my word. Begin now.

For Reflection

- *Which are your holy books? Have you honored them in any way? Have you marked any Web sites that inform and inspire you? Do you have other holy words that you honor? What might they be—letters, greeting cards, memorial cards, posters, others? How could they help you when you are searching for the right words?*

- *Do you have favorite prayers? Favorite Scripture passages?*

*How could you share these treasured words with someone
else? How could you help them to find their own holy
words?*

- *Emily Dickinson said "A word is dead / When it is said, /
Some say." She and you both know better. Are there any
words you want to bury? Any profane, critical or mean-
spirited words? Any old insults that still roll around in
your head or heart? How might you bury them?*

- *Examine your vocabulary for the five intelligible words:
prayer, praise, counsel, encouragement, confession. Which
words that you utter belong in these categories? Which
categories require you to find more words, new words,
stronger words?*

Closing Prayer

Sweet Jesus, is there anything sweeter than You?
To remember You
is more delightful than everything else.
Your name is joy;
it is the true gate of our salvation.
What else are You, Jesus, if not our Savior?
Be our Redeemer.
Give us the virtues of hope and love,
just as You have given us faith, our primary joy.
Give us the words that we need to praise you always.
With the help and through the prayers
of Your Mother.
You who are blessed throughout the ages. Amen.

—*Prayer of Saint Anthony*[17]

Notes

1 Emily Dickinson, *The Complete Poems of Emily Dickinson* (Boston: Little, Brown and Company, 1951), pp. 534-5.

2 *Life of St. Anthony*, p. 12.

3 Luke 8:11.

4 Wisdom 18:15.

5 *Ernest Hemingway: Selected Letters, 1917-1961*, edited by Carlos Baker (New York: Charles Scribner's Sons, 1981), p. 581.

6 John 1:1, 14a.

7 *Life of St. Anthony*, p. 11.

8 Caryll Houselander, *The Reed of God* (New York: Sheed & Ward, 1944), p. 3.

9 Marcil, p. 200.

10 1 Corinthians 14:19.

11 Marcil, p. 200.

12 1 Corinthians 1:5,7.

13 Matthew 5:24.

14 Marcil, p. 38.

15 Ephesians 4:31-32.

16 Habig, p. 107.

17 Jarmak, p. 157, adapted.

DAY SIX
Finding Unity

Coming Together in the Spirit

Those who see all creatures in themselves
And themselves in all creatures know no fear.
Those who see all creatures in themselves
And themselves in all creatures know no grief.
How can the multiplicity of life
Delude the one who sees its unity?

—The Upanishads[1]

Defining Our Thematic Context

In May, 1230, I returned to Padua. By Christmas, I was so aware of the Spirit moving that I determined to lead an area-wide Lenten retreat, preaching every day. Though this had never been done before, the crowds were so receptive and grew so large that I preached outdoors to accommodate them.

One of my biographers summarizes the season well: "These Lenten sermons became a religious revival not only for Padua but also for the surrounding district, since people came in great numbers to Padua from outlying villages and hamlets. To all, Anthony appeared as the herald of peace: His words achieved remarkable results. Quarrels were patched up, mortal enemies were

73

reconciled, poor debtors were released from prison and given their freedom, restitution was made of ill-gotten goods. Bad women renounced their evil manner of life, thieves and malefactors became honest men once more, and the whole public life of the citizens and the state once more became Christian in character."[2]

Pray with me now to know the unifying principle of your life. Pray to know the ways you can see yourself in all creatures and be at one with the universe. Let us pray to be heralds of peace.

Opening Prayer

Generous Lord of all creation,
You have surrounded us
with opposing forces
that pull and tug at us.
Yet you wish for us
not merely balance
but integration.

You want to knit us together
within ourselves,
within our families,
within creation.

I pray with you
that we all may be one.
I seek your face
in every face.
I seek your glory
in everything.

Retreat Session Six

Recognizing the
One True Face of Christ

I wish you could come with me to Padua, my adopted home, city that I love so much. As you seek to find your way in the world, it is a powerful spiritual exercise to picture the effects—the spiritual reverberations in the universe—of following the gospel path. Think now of the place where you live, the place to which you will return after this retreat. This is where you are called to be a herald of peace.

I was blessed to mark a year of peace in Padua and beyond, encompassing the entire March (border province) of Treviso. While its name and borders are now changed, the March embraced Verona to the west, moving up the spine of the Dolomites to the northern Alpine foothills, touching the Balkan border to the east, and not quite reaching to the Po River in the south. It was nearly the size of the state of Connecticut.

Some of the city I loved best is there yet. You can enter through the rounded stone arch which is one of the ancient city gates. Picture a Paduan, one of my peaceful people, waving to you from the iron-railed balcony above that arch. Admire the vividness of the red blossoms. Admire the clean laundry which also waves to you, hung on lines from balcony to balcony. Ah my Padua, that I loved.

The crowds shopping in Padua's squares today—the Piazza dei Frutti and the Piazza delle Erbe—remind me of the spiritually hungry people of 1231 who feasted daily on the word of God. It still amazes me that the message traveled and crowds continued to gather. Yet they did.

The word that I preached became flesh for me and for them.

I take such joy in remembering. It is the joy of the search for what is most deeply lost in us all, our own shadowy thickets, our borderlands. It is the joy of discovering that we have within us the map to our treasure and the compass to locate the place of its concealment. We can act on our words. They can take the shape of love.

I offer four experiences of my own, experiences of being moved to act by the gospel in this blessed season. May they suggest to you the lines and locations of your own treasure map, your personal scenario for action.

Find Christ in Your Debtors and Your Creditors

Three ways to pray present themselves in Scripture: "interior prayer, vocal prayer and bodily prayer.... About bodily prayer, the Apostle says, 'Pray without ceasing.'[3] A person does not cease praying who does not cease doing good."[4] To pray with my body, to act as I had preached, to be single-minded, became my constant call this Lent.

While my daily sermons attracted both rich and poor, there was no middle class. As money became the medium of exchange and was needed by farmers and artisans, they often went into debt at high interest rates. Then, if they fell ill or were injured, they might need more money, or an extension, risking what little they owned as collateral. Sometimes they saw no way out and defaulted.

The law of Padua was life imprisonment for failure to pay debts, with no concern for motive or circumstances. Proud men tried to cling to the old ways, bartering, trading, avoiding cash transactions. Sometimes they managed, but barely. Others took the risk and lost. Women and children were evicted from their little country homes. The city and its merchants were prospering, but my poor, the poor who were Christ incarnate, were populating the debtors' prisons.

I decided to risk my own capital. I had the goodwill of the city's leaders who saw that all of Padua benefited from the penitence, the kindness, the respect for others, that the gospel inspired. I drafted an amendment to the city statutes. It was a small mercy but one that gave hope. The city fathers recorded it on the books thus: "At the request of the honorable and holy brother, Anthony, the confessor of the Order of Friars Minor, no one, whether a debtor or a guarantor, is to be deprived of his personal freedom in the future if he is incapable of paying. In such a case, he can be deprived of his property, but not of his personal freedom."[5]

My beloved Padua adopted this amendment and moved in a good direction. I felt I was not only being an advocate for debtors, but I was also helping the wealthy to see that no law should lay a heavier burden on the poor. I appreciate the biographer who calls this legal reform "the greatest of the miracles which he [Anthony] worked in his lifetime."[6]

You humor me to listen to this ancient Italian history, but now I put to you this challenge: Take out your credit and debit records. Who "owes you one"? And in whose debt have you placed yourself?

I once preached on the gospel story of the clever bookkeeper, who had been wasting his master's wealth and was about to be let go. I find much wisdom there for debtors and creditors alike. Luke writes, "Summoning his master's debtors one by one, he [the bookkeeper] asked the first, 'How much do you owe my master?' He answered, 'A hundred jars of olive oil.' He said to him, 'Take your bill, sit down quickly, and make it fifty.' Then he asked another, 'How much do you owe?' He replied,

'A hundred containers of wheat.' He said to him, 'Take your bill and make it eighty.'"[7]

Now I ask you as I asked in my *Sermones*:

"How much do you owe?"—meaning, to what degree must you love your neighbor in the Lord? He will answer: In the measure of "a hundred measures of wheat," that is, the love of friend and enemy, in and through the Lord; and if it be necessary, to be ready to give my life for my neighbor.

However, since I am carnal and weak, I cannot attain to such a perfection of love for my neighbor. And then the manager ought to tell him: "Since you are not yet ready to offer your life for your neighbor," for the moment, "take your bill and write eighty."

"'Take your bill,' that is, prepare your soul for loving your neighbor, 'and write eighty,' meaning, teach him if he is in error, and refresh him if he is weak. Keep this bill always before your eyes, and whenever you see others, symbolically write eighty on them; then when you see it written, you will be reminded to love them. If you read it this way, the bill itself will pave the way for you to merit an eternal reward."[8]

I repeat my question from the perspective of a spiritual resource manager: How much do you owe? To whom are you indebted? I owe so much to my parents, who sent me to the cathedral school in Lisbon, who had me baptized, who walked in the way of faith and inspired me to enter religious life. I owe my teachers, I owe the humble friars who came begging at Coimbra's monastery door. I owe the Cathari, who challenged me to be holy, body and soul, without distancing myself from either the Church or the people.

Take out your bill now and consider how you will pay your debts to family, to Church, to your civic community, to the earth itself. What laws are unjust? How can you influence custom and behavior where you work, where you live? You have a lot of charges on your spiritual credit card. It is time to consider how you will pay!

To claim your spiritual reward, you must also release those indebted to you—or, at least, take their bills and mark them down! Who owes you? Do you bill your children with "oughts" and "shoulds" beyond their ability to act? Do you think your spouse owes you for all that you do to make your home comfortable and welcoming? Or are you owed respect for contributing financially? Do you think your workplace owes you more than you receive? Take out the ledger of your debtors and mark them down to eighty—if you cannot forgive their debt entirely.

Let this be your own private Lenten reform, a new ledger, a "year of jubilee" in which "you proclaim liberty throughout the land to all its inhabitants."[9] Listen for the cry of the poor in your life.

Find Christ in Your Captives and Your Jailers

When I had settled my debts, such as they were for this poor Franciscan, I saw that injustice still lingered in the March of Treviso. The shadow cast by Ezzelino da Romano was a long one. Ezzelino and I were about the same age, but his path had led him not to peace but to political intrigue, armed battle and assassinations. He was a leader of a political party that favored the interests of the German emperor Frederick II over those of the Roman pope, Gregory IX.

Ezzelino kept his headquarters in the commune of Verona, at the foot of the Brenner Pass. Running from the north into Italy's heart, this was a route which Ezzelino controlled.

After I had celebrated Holy Week and Easter in Padua, I was asked to take "bodily prayer" another step—a step toward the Verona of Ezzelino. I was swollen with edema, but I saw that this was an opportunity to exert spiritual influence where other power held little hope for success. Ezzelino was "the most hated and feared man in Italy"[10] at the time and he had held Count Riccardo—a Paduan from an opposing party—prisoner for several years.

I walked over fifty miles to Verona alone so there is no witness to tell you of my encounter. I knew that Ezzelino killed without compunction and that I had only the power of the gospel to protect me. While I had succeeded in effecting a change in Paduan law, I was unable to effect a change in this man's heart. I will only say that the count remained in Ezzelino's clutches. "[T]he devil whose name is death...uses the cruel tyrant of this world...."[11] I left Verona alive but with a tired and aching heart and body.

Who are your captors? Have your resigned yourself to imprisonment? Have you imprisoned yourself in solitary confinement, not extending yourself beyond the narrow borders of self-interest? Are you imprisoned by what you own, protecting yourself with security systems, fences and other barricades? Are you held captive by your own fears?

Are you, rather, the warden in a prison of your own construction? Do you have power which you use to oppress? Have you established unjust boundaries that exclude people of other cultures, political or religious beliefs? Are there people to whom you choose not to speak? Do you judge and sentence others without mercy?

Isaiah says, "The spirit of the Lord God is upon me, because the Lord has anointed me; / he has sent me to bring good news to the oppressed, to bind up the brokenhearted, / to proclaim liberty to the captives, and release to the prisoners; / to proclaim the year of the LORD's favor...."[12] And, I, Anthony, believe that you have taken prisoners whom you must release. Captive and keeper of the keys are both in chains until both are free.

Find Christ on the Edges

Today, what Italians called the Marches or borderlands could be called the Margins. Its motley citizens are indeed the marginalized, people falling through the cracks, as you say, people on the edge of public consciousness, people exempted from the demands of public conscience.

In Paduan law, I upheld the poor. Confronting Ezzelino, I defended the nobility. Reaching out and preaching to the outlanders, I hoped to effect a transformation in the stratified Italian culture.

Here I believe I must explain myself. When you read my *Sermones*, you see my outlines, my broad interpretations, my universal applications. They provide an example, a pattern, an approach. The people on the margins flocked to the open fields to hear me break open the gospel not because I was universal but because I was specific. I addressed their native intelligence, their instincts for spiritual survival, their longing for a heavenly realm beyond Citadella (the Paduan defensive fortress) or Verona or any place built and defended on the broad plains of the Po River.

I delighted in the presence of the border dwellers. It made Padua into a paradise for me, to see such a mingling. As a preacher, I was challenged to reach into my store and bring out something for everyone. Jesus had supplied the text; mine was simply the application. I took as my own the words of the Old Testament prophet: "Go through the city [I recognized the city as my Padua]...and put a mark on the foreheads of those who sigh and groan over all the abominations that are committed in it."[13] It was my task, in the name of Jesus, to "'inscribe the tau,'" that is, the sign of the cross and the memory of his passion, 'on the foreheads,' that is, deep within the minds of penitents who weep in contrition, and who are sorrowful in confessing 'all the abominations' which they have done or which others are doing."[14]

This had been Francis of Assisi's delight, to claim the whole world under the sign of the tau. A letter of the alphabet became also the cross under which I could rally my "weary multitude." The penance I required of those who sought forgiveness was that they set Padua's own prisoners free, that they make restitution for any bribery, extortion or fraud, that those forgiven "go...do not sin again."[15]

As the days of Lent passed, these penitents, marked with ashes at Lent's beginning and with the spiritual tau as they experienced forgiveness, had little reason to think themselves separate from one another. They shared their loaves and fishes as though we were the congregation of the Sermon on the Mount. We all experienced Beatitude.

And who is in your peripheral vision only? Who is on the margins of your life? Where can you go to be with people from all walks of life? Do you go there or do you avoid the parks, the market, the public gathering places of your city? Have you walked or driven through your area's poorest neighborhood? Why not? What actions could you take so that the "abominations" of your city could be marked with the tau? How could you come to see the Christ in your urban clinics, to serve Christ in his many disguises?

How will you define mercy at your own margins? "It is said of elephants that if at any time they fight in battle, they take good care of their wounded. For they gather the tired and the injured into the center of the herd [away from the margins]. In the same way, you should receive into the center of your love the wearied and the wounded...."[16]

Find Christ Everywhere

Peace was difficult to come by in the Italy of my day, when the city-states were often at war. You may remember that Francis of Assisi was injured in just such a war before his conversion. So, the peace in Padua and its environs felt to many like a welcome miracle. It was a peace to which everyone in the Marches made a contribution. While many people must cooperate to build peace, one or two can quickly disturb it.

I have written of peace as "three-fold": temporal peace (with others), peace of heart (within) and eternal peace (with God). I experienced it as a progression in the life of Padua and came to experience hints of eternal peace while still on this earth. Love and peace became synonyms in my experience, just as the Hindus had written in their ancient mystical document, the Upanishads. I knew neither fear nor grief.

I was at peace before the city's lawmakers and before Ezzelino. The same peace extended across the fields as I preached to crowds of thousands. (Some say the numbers reached thirty thousand.) I only know I felt the presence of many, lifted my voice to speak of peace and felt the blessing returned to me in "good measure, pressed down, shaken together, running over."[17]

In the Year of Peace, intellect, spirit and feeling often moved as one in me. So did I lack a sense of separation from others. I believe this is the experience that the Cistercian Thomas Merton was describing when he stood on a street corner in downtown Louisville, Kentucky, and felt one with all the shoppers. He wrote, "I was suddenly overwhelmed with the realization that I loved all those people, that they were mine and I theirs, that we could not be alien to one another even though we were total strangers.... There are no strangers!"[18]

Such mystical moments are experiences of the Body of Christ. You are meant to know such moments. Teilhard de Chardin prayed and I pray with him now: "Take up in your hands, Lord, and bless this universe that is destined to sustain and fulfill the plenitude of your being among us."[19] In its plenitude, we rest as one.

I once wrote, "The many facets of Jesus Christ are the Church's good prelates and all the saints, for through them altogether we know the one true face of Christ."[20]

For Reflection

- **Find Christ in Your Debtors and Your Creditors.** *Focus on one individual to whom you experience a debt—of honor, of gratitude, of money. Make a plan to pay your debt. You may prefer to focus on someone who feels indebted to you—financially or emotionally. Consider how you might forgive them their debt.*

- **Find Christ in Your Captives and Your Jailers.** *Identify someone you hold captive and someone who holds you fast in some area of your life. As you consider how to release your own captive, imagine the same happening to you in the area of your own imprisonment. Can you request freedom?*

- **Find Christ on the Edges.** *Locate the margins of your community. Name them and consider how you might act to be a peacemaker, a unifier, in a marginal area. Perhaps the* *margin you locate is* more *prosperous than your own neighborhood. If you feel alienated or excluded from it, it is marginal to your life. What contribution do you have to make in such a place?*

■ **Find Christ Everywhere.** *At your next celebration of the Eucharist, use this prayer of thanksgiving after communion. Every communicant will hear the words, "Body of Christ." As you hear this truth proclaimed again and again, respond in your heart, "Amen." That Amen not only affirms that the bread has become the Bread of Life, but that the person receiving is part of the Body of Christ in which you believe.*

Closing Prayer

A favorite blessing used by Saint Anthony against evils of all kinds, including the violence that destroys peace, was to make the sign of the cross as he said these words:

Behold the Cross of the Lord!
Begone, you evil powers!
The Lion of the tribe of Juda,
the Root of David,
has conquered.
Alleluia!

> —*The Brief, or Blessing,*
> *of Saint Anthony*[21]

Notes

[1] The Isha Upanishad, "The Inner Ruler," in *God Makes the River to Flow*, edited by Eknath Easwaran (Berkeley, Ca.: Nilgiri Press,

1991), p. 83.

[2] Clasen, p. 93.

[3] 1 Thessalonians 5:17.

[4] Marcil, p. 214.

[5] Hardik, p. 36.

[6] Hardik, p. 37.

[7] Luke 16:5-7.

[8] Jarmak, pp. 214-215.

[9] Leviticus 25:13, 10.

[10] Vernon Bartlett, *Northern Italy* (New York: Hastings House, 1973), p. 132.

[11] Marcil, p. 124.

[12] Isaiah 61:1-3.

[13] Ezekiel 9:3-4.

[14] Marcil, p. 128.

[15] John 8:11

[16] Marcil, p. 97.

[17] Luke 6:38.

[18] Thomas Merton, *Conjectures of a Guilty Bystander* (Garden City, N.Y.: Doubleday, 1966), p. 142.

[19] Pierre Teilhard de Chardin, *The Prayer of the Universe* (New York: Harper & Row, 1965), p. 159.

[20] Marcil, p. 111.

[21] Clasen, p. 84.

DAY SEVEN
Finding Completion

Coming Together in the Spirit

Lent-laden death-deprived
like a sea-weary sailor looking landward
I squeeze hope from spring juice.
What I want is Easter.

—John McNamee, S.J.[1]

While I was never a poet, I have looked over your
shoulders and found that this modern poet, John
McNamee, wrote a poem that describes the experience of
my final Lent in this life. A retreat is a little Lent. What I
want—for you—is Lent's glorious ending, Easter!

Defining Our Thematic Context

I want you to "squeeze hope" from every hour we
have spent together. I see you "squeezing" all that is good
and blessed from every day of your life—moving
forward, situating yourself in a holy place and taking
time to be in that place, seeking balance wherever you
are, speaking with power and acting with grace.

In every beginning, we are to keep the end in mind.
In every search, we are to visualize the treasure. As I
concluded the season of Lent in 1231, I was indeed "a sea-

weary sailor looking landward." I moved my meager belongings to Camposampiero, a smaller town not far from Padua.

My friend Count Tiso had a forest in Camposampiero. I found in his forest a walnut tree of "extraordinary beauty.... [T]he place offered suitable solitude and the kind of rest which is conducive to contemplation."[2] Kind Tiso built me a tree house, a refuge reminiscent of the cave at Montepaolo (the Mountain of Paul), with the difference that I had gone down into the cave but now I climbed up into the giant tree, "near to heaven."[3] Let us climb now, together.

Opening Prayer

Lord Jesus,
you sought the hills and the heights
to express your message
and your meaning.
From the Sermon on the Mount
to the sermon on Calvary,
you asked us to look up and learn
and then to join you.

Help me to squeeze the hope
from every hill and valley.
Show me the high way
to glory.

May the tree rise up
which I can climb to you.

Retreat Session Seven
Squeezing Hope From Spring Juice

When we met on Day One, I began to trace the movement of the Spirit in my life, using words from the Holy Scriptures to describe the graces I have received. I have continued to illuminate and understand my life through the Word of God. I hope I have led you to find your life expressed and clarified in the pages of the Bible, to return to its pages and find there your autobiography.

Today, I repeat that the life of Jesus, my life and yours have much in common. When I look in the Gospels, I claim its verses as my own—to comfort, to promise or to challenge me. I believe we can squeeze hope from their spring juice together: four gifts named rest, growth, inspiration and treasure.

'May a season of refreshment be granted you'

The name *Camposampiero* means "the village of Peter." In my writings, I have revealed my insatiable interest in etymology, the roots of words. The deep meaning of each syllable, I was convinced, contributed to a fuller understanding of God's universe. And so, I came for a "time of refreshing"[4] to the village of Peter. To me, *Peter* implies the beginning, the basis, a place to anchor oneself. Camposampiero was all that to me—and more. I have come full circle—from my quiet refuge in Montepaolo (Paul's mountain) to another blessed retreat in Peter's village.

In the First Letter of Peter, then, it does not surprise me to read a reflection of my intuition about this short journey to Camposampiero: "The end of all things is near; therefore be serious and discipline yourselves for the sake of your prayers."[5]

The town itself is calm. Clare's Order has a monastery there now and one effect of their prayerful presence is to quiet the entire surrounding area. I am glad that the place where I began my conversation with Sister Death still has woods which include nut-bearing trees and a space to cultivate the spring of silence.

An author of your time, Carol Shields, has written a novel about the seasons of a family's life. In a chapter called "Illness and Decline," her character Daisy Flett enters the same season of life which I am recalling now. Shields describes it well: "All she's [Daisy Flett] trying to do is keep things straight in her head. To keep the weight of her memories evenly distributed. To hold the chapters of her life in order. She feels a new tenderness growing for certain moments; they're like beads on a string, and the string is wearing out.... Words are more and more required. And the question arises: what is the story of a life?.... She needs a quiet place in which to think about this immensity."[6]

For myself, although things are straight in my head, I, too, am wearing out and need "a quiet place in which to think about this immensity," to worry my own beads moment by moment, to consider the story of my life and its order.

On our second day together, we spoke about staking a claim to holy ground and keeping vigil there. I also emphasized that you would need to "camp out" some times and simply be where you are. I am returning to that theme of our retreat and to that need in my life.

How is it different now? No one followed me into my cave ten years ago. I was an anonymous hermit blessed with a place of retreat. Now, perhaps, I am more like you, coming from the bustle of a busy public life. My kind biographer says that "suitable solitude" was mine, but the many paintings of this time in my life portray a different picture.

A seventeenth-century fresco in the little chapel at Camposampiero is typical. I am preaching from the tree to a crowd including women with children and well-dressed men. The crowd extends as far as the eye can see.

Please accept this image as my most profound experience of holy ground. I had the courage to express my need for seclusion and went to extraordinary lengths—climbing up into a tree—to claim it. From this perch, however, I was willing to look out with compassion and continue my work with the people of Padua. I gave them the fruits of the tree in which I grew so close to heaven.

You have experienced with me a small season of refreshment. Just as spring follows winter, such a season will come your way again, as soon as tomorrow, or as distant as your calendar seems to require. Remain calm. Be ready to take extraordinary measures to "think about this immensity," to "squeeze hope from spring juice."

'You can tell a tree by its fruit'

Just as the Gospels are also our biography, the liturgical year is also our calendar. On it you will find the days of your life in the guise of the feasts of Jesus and his saints. In 1231, I celebrated the Feast of Ascension in a tree! I laugh to myself when I recall it, but it was not as far-fetched as it may sound to your modern ears.

It was a damp season throughout the March of Treviso. It seemed foolish to build a little hermitage in the woods and become stiff as a planed board myself from the moist earth beneath my bones! It may stretch your credulity to think of me, a grown man, a respected man, a dignified man, hiding, as it were, in a tree house. I would rather have you entertained, delighted. It will only increase my own delight.

In my sturdy walnut perch, I cannot help but consider the significance of a tree in my spiritual history. From the tree of Genesis[7] to the tree of the cross[8] to the tree of life in the Book of Revelation,[9] I am one with the trees.

I once wrote that "a good tree consists of five things: roots, trunk, branches, leaves and fruit. A good tree is a symbol for a righteous person who, in order to be good, must also possess five things: the roots of humility, the trunk of obedience, the branches of charity, the leaves of holy preaching and fruit, that is, the sweetness of heavenly contemplation."[10] I am in the season of pre-Pentecostal waiting. It is my time of sweetness after the decades-long stretches of seeking, suffering and stretching toward the sky. As the Book of Proverbs says, "The fruit of the righteous is a tree of life."[11] I taste it.

Do I suggest that you conclude your retreat by tree-climbing or camping? Perhaps. I want you to determine what drastic measures it would take for you to bear fruit in due season. Consider your harvest. "You can tell a tree by its fruit."[12] Have you experienced fruitful seasons in your life? What conditions have supported your harvest? Have you allowed the dormancy or rest that allows strength to gather within? What promises to blossom now as you consider the seventh day, the day of rest?

All this came to me as I sat in the largest walnut tree of the forest of Camposampiero, considering the season of the Church, marking the days between Ascension and Pentecost. I am well positioned for an event that comes "from heaven."[13] You, too, need to find the nest in which you can absorb the sun, soak up the energy of soil and water, grow and bear fruit. "Blessed are those who wash their robes, so that they will have the right to the tree of life and may enter the city [heavenly Jerusalem] by the gates!"[14]

'The Mighty One has done great things for me'

In my tree-refuge, I had the liberty to continue my work on sermons for the feasts of the saints. I have left you many, but I did not live to complete this volume. I recall with great satisfaction, however, that I did leave sermons for the feasts of the Queen of All Saints, Mary.

As I considered, despite my illness, the feasts of the saints, my mind and heart were continually called to contemplate Mary. It was as though my tree became an upper room, in which I waited with Mary and the Apostles for the coming of the Spirit.

Mary speaks to us in Scripture only six times. I have combed these passages to learn her virtues and to gather strength for my own life—and death. Two passages are from John (2:3 and 2:5). Four passages are from Luke's Gospel (1:34, 1:38, 1:46 ff. and 2:48). From these Scriptures, I have numbered her virtues as the six branches of a candlestick or the six leaves of a lily.[15]

I constantly found her virtue prefigured in the writings of the Hebrew Scriptures as well. I compared her fruitfulness to the fruitfulness of the trees described in Leviticus 23:40, the trees from whose branches the Israelites constructed booths or tents to celebrate the harvest.[16] She was the first booth in which the Lord Jesus was to dwell, I saw. I wanted to be such a tent myself now, as I prepared for the harvest to come.

I turned to her song of "exultation for the blessings given her," the Magnificat. It was my daily prayer at the evening hour of Vespers, but it also became my prayer for every hour of the day and night. "The Mighty One has done great things for me."[17] Here I was, a lowly person in a high place, rejoicing just as she had done before me. Her canticle, filled with allusions to earlier holy books, was my pattern for looking back always to see the new in the old, to find the present and past linked in the eternal mind of God, to experience that link now extending to promises coming close to fulfillment in my life. At the very end, as I lay dying, I began to sing a hymn to Mary. "O Glorious Lady, fairest Queen," it began.[18]

And it concluded, "O Mother dear of grace divine, God's mercy for us sinners plead, protect us from the enemy, in life's last hour to heaven lead."[19] When my dear friend, Friar Luke, asked me what my eyes now saw, I was able to answer, "I see my Lord."[20]

I saw him as Mary first saw him, the little one allowing himself to be needy, to be loved, to be held close. I had imagined this infant nestled in my arms so many times, as I crooned the words, "My spirit rejoices in God my Savior."[21] Now I was the one to nestle, to be held, to look up and see.

My death came just after Pentecost, the birth of the Church. In quick succession, I had entered into the fullness of Lenten penance, Easter joy, Ascension longing and Pentecostal fire. "The Holy Spirit has come over me" and now I come full circle to birth once more.

It is Mary who taught us how to prepare for this birth, this entrance into a new realm of life eternal. "The Mighty One has done great things for me," she sang. This time of ending is a time to remember these great things and, in remembering to take heart and give thanks. What are the great things God has done in you? Do you see the Lord? Where? How? How does Mary help you to see Jesus?

'Rejoice with me, I have found the coin!'

Early on the first day of our journey together, I suggested "Search and you will find"[22] as our scriptural motif. Today, I suggest its corollary, "Rejoice with me, for I have found the coin that I had lost."[23]

I have spoken to you as an eyewitness from the place of rejoicing, the place where all that has been lost is restored. My repeated invitation to you: Let us "rediscover the face of the Lord that we have lost, let us light a lamp and diligently sweep the house."[24]

We have been sweeping, haven't we? Sometimes what we seek is lost only to our consciousness, plainly visible when we find first the time and place for prayerful discovery. Sometimes, in the seeking, we find other treasures we had not even missed—or known to miss! It is a privilege to be God's spiritual assistant in this journey of seeking and finding.

Matthew's Gospel speaks of a treasure which sounds larger than the silver piece we have been seeking, though it is undoubtedly in the same chest of spiritual jewels and heavenly gold. "For where your treasure is, there your heart will be also."[25] When I preached on this subject, I added, "God seeks no other part of a human being, loves nothing in us as much as the heart, in which is the law of love."[26]

I believe that this truth works in both directions. If you find your treasure, you will find which chambers of your heart need sweeping to make room for greater treasures still. If you find your heart (or allow it to be found by God), you will have a chest in which to store your treasures safely. You will not so easily misplace what was lost and now is found.

Rejoice, be happy, then, in the seeking, finding, sorting, letting go, acquiring and praising the Giver of all. I assure you that you know the way. I assure you that, to regain your bearings on the path, to squeeze hope, to remember the way, you need only recall the treasure you have seen from your tree house of retreat.

For Reflection

- When will you seek a season of refreshment? When will you consider "the weight of your memories and distribute or redistribute them? When will you take time to "squeeze hope from spring juice?" Pray and mark your calendar.

- What is your image of spiritual growth? Do you have a tree, a bush, a perennial flower? Do you have anything growing in your house, even within your holy ground? Name your memories of natural splendor, like Anthony's walnut tree. Consider ways to keep powerful images before your inner eye—photo-prayer albums, posters, framed photos or paintings or a membership in a botanical garden. Use the poem "Renascence" by Edna St. Vincent Millay as a prayer of praise and connection with creation.

- Pray the Magnificat and the Canticle of Hannah.[27] Attend a communal Vespers service to pray the Magnificat in a community. Mark the next festival of Mary with Mass. Pray the Rosary. Consider your own joyful, sorrowful and glorious mysteries. Feel a new "tenderness growing for certain moments; they're like beads on a string...."

- Prepare a litany of praise for the treasures you have found. Name them: "For the park bench which I claim as holy ground, I thank you, God." Consider a litany of petitions for the treasures you intend to seek: "For the courage to claim the time my soul requires, I beg your grace and mercy, Lord."

Closing Prayer

To the ends of the earth...
proclaim the word of joy...:
"Ask, that your joy may be full."

Proclaim it not only to the just
who are in the Church's midst,
but to the outer bounds of the earth...,
that is, outside the precepts of the Lord,
which are for us the bounds within which
    we must live.
Let them hear the word of joy
so that they might obtain the full joy
which has no bounds.
May Jesus Christ lead us to this joy. Amen.

                —Prayer of Saint Anthony[28]

Notes

[1] John McNamee, "Easter Longing," *Clay Vessels and Other Poems* (Kansas City, Mo.: Sheed & Ward, 1995), p. 5.

[2] *Life of St. Anthony*, p. 20.

[3] *Life of St. Anthony*, p. 20.

[4] Acts 3:20.

[5] 1 Peter 4:7.

[6] Carol Shields, *The Stone Diaries* (New York: Penguin Books, 1993), p. 340.

[7] Genesis 2:9.

[8] Acts 5:30.

[9] Revelation 22:14.

[10] Jarmak, p. 196.

[11] Proverbs 11:30.

[12] Matthew 7:20.

[13] Acts 2:2.

[14] Revelation 22:14.

[15] Rohr, p. 76.

[16] Rohr, p. 77.

[17] Luke 1:49.

[18] Clasen, p. 99

[19] Clasen, p. 100.
[20] *Life of St. Anthony*, p. 24.
[21] Luke 1:47.
[22] Matthew 7:7.
[23] Luke 15:9.
[24] Marcil, p. 215.
[25] Matthew 6:21.
[26] Marcil, p. 197.
[27] 1 Samuel 1:9-20.
[28] Marcil, p. 194.

Going Forth to Live the Theme

I have a reputation as "the saint of the miracles." You may have noticed that I made no mention of the many miracles attributed to me, some the stuff of legend during my lifetime, others documented after my death.

Each day, people count on me for the miracles of finding lost objects, safeguarding the mail, protecting those at sea and, more extraordinarily, finding spouses.

To the extent that God is honored, I am pleased to be the instrument of all these miracles. But I wish you to know the pleasure as well. As you continue the searches that have been outlined in this retreat as well as other searches of the heart and spirit you have been led to name, miracles can be expected. I urge you to anticipate them, to honor them, to praise the God of miracles and wonders who is active in your life.

I offer you a song to accompany the odyssey of your own miracles. Called "Ordinary Miracles," it concludes with these words: "...endless possibilities right before our eyes. See the way a miracle multiplies. Hope can spring eternally, plant it and it grows. Love is all that's necessary, love in its extr'ordinary way makes ordinary miracles every blessed day."[1]

Jesus was tempted in the desert, and on the cross, to work miracles for his own benefit. I believe we are all tempted to use our powers to increase our comfort, our peace and our personal harmony. The miracles which I would inspire in you are miracles of extension, of connection, of union. Believe in miracles, God's on your behalf, and God's power working through you to touch others. You, too, can heal, forgive, nourish—and find what is lost.

Notes

[1] Words by Alan Bergman and Marilyn Bergman, "Ordinary Miracles," *Forty Songs for a Better World* (Milwaukee, Wis.: Hal Leonard Corporation, 1995), pp. 134-8.

Deepening Your Acquaintance

To learn more about Saint Anthony of Padua, consider these resources:

Books

Clasen, Sophronius, O.F.M., translated by Ignatius Brady, O.F.M. *St. Anthony, Doctor of the Church*. Chicago: Franciscan Herald Press, 1973.

Foley, Leonard, O.F.M., and Norman Perry, O.F.M. *St. Anthony of Padua: The Story of His Life and Popular Devotions*. Cincinnati: St. Anthony Messenger Press, 1993.

Hardick, Lothar, O.F.M., translated by Fr. Zachary Hayes. *Anthony of Padua: Proclaimer of the Gospel*. Paterson, N.J.: St. Anthony's Guild, 1994.

Jarmak, Claude M., O.F.M., Conv. *If You Seek Miracles: Reflections of Saint Anthony of Padua*. Padua, Italy: Edizioni Messaggero Padova, 1998.

_____. *Saint Anthony: Herald of the Good News*. Ellicott City, Md.: Conventual Franciscan Friars, 1995.

Nugent, Madeline Pecora, S.F.O. *Saint Anthony: Words of Fire, Life of Light*. Boston: Pauline Books & Media, 1995.

_____. *Praying With Anthony of Padua*. Winona, Minn.: Saint Mary's Press, 1996.

Poloniato, Fr. Livio, O.F.M., Conv. *St. Anthony of Padua: Seek First His Kingdom.* Ellicott City, Md.: Conventual Franciscan Friars, 1988.

_____. *Praise to You Lord: Prayers of St. Anthony.* Padua, Italy: Edizioni Messaggero Padova, 1986.

Letter of the Ministers General of the Franciscan Family. *Anthony, Man of the Gospel.* Saint Louis, Mo.: O.F.M. English-Speaking Conference, 1995.

Video

Castellani, Leandro. *Anthony of Padua: Gospel and Charity.* TVC Productions, Rome, Italy, 1995 (Distributed in the United States by the Anthonian Association of the Friends of St. Anthony, 101 St. Anthony Drive, Mount St. Francis, Indiana 47146).